FORWARD

BY LISA OLSEN, MS, CWCA

Throughout my career, I've always been an advocate of continuous learning. I realized how important it is to develop and grow as an administrative professional when I was promoted to support the CEO of a healthcare company early in my career.

Let's call it what it was: *scary!* I had been in the assistant role for a few years, but stepping into the world of a CEO is different. I didn't know what to expect. I was not sure I had all the tools I needed to be successful. This CEO was new to the role as well.

Don't get me wrong. I knew this was an opportunity, but I was afraid too. *Very* afraid. At that point in time, I didn't exactly want to follow the "feel the fear and do it anyway" routine. Nope. Not this assistant. Thankfully, I snapped out of it and got busy getting some help.

I had attended one or two conferences previously and gained some valuable information, but I wanted more. I began my quest to find resources that offered specific content that could help me rise to the challenge I was facing. I searched the World Wide Web (which is what we called it back in those days!) and came across a blog called The EA Toolbox by Chrissy Scivicque. Wow! I had discovered gold. Or at least, gold nuggets of solid information. I often found myself reading the blog posts, nodding my head and saying out loud, "She gets it!"

I was so impressed with Chrissy's clear, direct, and content-rich material, I sent her an email and let her know how much her ideas were helping me nourish my career as an EA. It was true. Her blog topics were focused and well-written, covering relevant topics that got to the nuts and bolts of the *why* and the *how*, not just the *what*. She tackled the topics that are the core of this career, many of which are also included in this book.

I started following Chrissy and, over the next few years, we continued to correspond by email and eventually by phone. We had long conversations about the administrative career and our own career journeys as trainers and professional speakers, and we shared how we hoped our paths would one day cross in person. How grateful I am that we did eventually meet at an Office Dynamics Conference where we were both speaking. We've been colleagues and good friends ever since.

I've continued to rely on Chrissy's expertise and experience and have attended many of her training programs. She was also one of our most popular guest speakers at our annual retreat for assistants, where she presented on being a proactive professional. The session really knocked the socks off our attendees. We were picking up socks for hours!

Elevation is at the core of continuous development. To elevate signifies upward movement and action. We have to heighten our confidence, rise to challenges, advance our skillsets, and magnify the role. It's a continual process of growth. Chrissy's experience as an administrative professional, certified career coach, and certified project manager, as well as her outstanding training programs qualify her to write this book all about the concept of career elevation.

Thank you, Chrissy, for your commitment to helping administrative professionals elevate. After reading this book, everyone will be nodding their heads saying, "She gets it!"

Lisa Olsen, MS, CWCA
ADMIN TO ADMIN

PREFACE

In March 2020, I was roughly 80 percent done with this book and looking forward to an early summer publication date. Little did I know our world was about to be turned upside down.

The COVID-19 pandemic impacted every human on the planet in dramatic ways. No one escaped the chaos it inflicted, personally and professionally. Certainly some suffered more than others, but we all experienced *some* level of trauma.

As I write this, it's been just over a year since the first shutdowns in the U.S. In that period of time, I made a conscious choice to postpone the publication of this book. So I filed the manuscript away and didn't touch it for the rest of 2020. In hindsight, I think that was a smart decision.

The administrative field, like many other professional fields, has been profoundly impacted by the pandemic. Our global admin community has been forever altered. However, the long-term effects are still unknown. It's reasonable to expect certain things, like remote work and virtual events, are here to stay. But to what degree, remains to be seen. We have, essentially, tapped into a whole new world of possibilities for support staff—and this is likely to have both positive and negative consequences in the years to come. Some people and roles will benefit, others will not. But there's no going back now.

Just recently, I pulled out this nearly completed manuscript and read it again with fresh eyes. Only ten months had passed, but it seemed like a lifetime. As I read, I was struck by one overwhelming thought: *This book is needed now more than ever.*

In the past year, we have all been forced to "elevate" in every aspect of our lives—at home, at work, in our communities. We've had to lift ourselves up in ways we never knew possible, and in doing so, we discovered new depths of capability. We learned new technology overnight, created processes and systems that never existed, figured out how to home school our kids *and* work remotely *at the same time*, rearranged thousands of hours of travel and meetings, and managed to somehow keep our families fed and our businesses running when everything around us was unsteady, uncertain, and sometimes downright terrifying.

Administrative professionals around the world stepped up, figured it out, and made it work.

But hey, that's nothing new.

Now, you get to step up *for yourself.* You get to take this newly tapped capacity for infinite growth and this newly revealed world of possibility, and create your career future. There has never been a better time to be an administrative professional. We are in the midst of a very exciting evolution.

Of course, as with any evolution, only the fittest will survive.

This is a perfect moment in time to reevaluate your role, realign with your purpose, and recommit to your career—to enhance your professional "fitness" so you're in the best possible position for the future. This is a moment to embrace your own personal evolution.

I hope this book will be a catalyst in that process.

I am dubious of anyone who claims to know with certainty how the pandemic will impact our field or the workplace in general over the coming years. But there's one thing I know for certain: It *will* have a lasting impact on each of us.

What we do from here—with all that we've learned and all that we've experienced—will determine what that impact is.

1

INTRODUCTION

When I was a little girl, I used to play *Secretary*. I'd put on my mother's high heels, pull out the old rotary phone my grandmother gave me, and set up my blue plastic typewriter—the kind that had keys that would clump up and stick to the ribbon. I could spend hours transferring imaginary calls to imaginary executives, banging out very important messages, and organizing my father's junk mail in orderly stacks beside my bed.

Secretary was always my favorite game.

I remember those days fondly and still get a kick out of the fact that I had such an early love for the idea of administrative work (however primitive my childhood idea of it was). I find it fitting that I spent much of my career as a young adult in admin, and today, as an international speaker and trainer, I specialize in working with support professionals and administrative teams. I have developed a profound respect, admiration and appreciation for the role, which is far more complex and nuanced than my seven-year-old brain could have ever imagined. It is both extremely challenging and extremely rewarding work, and, as my young-self predicted, it is work I truly love.

It is my love for the administrative profession that led me to write this book. In fact, my passion for this field has been the driving force throughout my career—from the three years in college when I worked as a receptionist in an optometry office to my final admin role ten years later as the Executive Assistant to the Senior Managing Partner of an elite wealth management firm. At every step, I saw the profound impact a strong administrative partner could have on an organization, and I was proud to play that critical role.

At the same time, I came to understand that many of my administrative colleagues didn't feel the same way.

Some saw their admin work as a "stepping stone" to something bigger and better. They treated their time in the role like a career purgatory of sorts.

Others saw it as just a job—a paycheck in exchange for hours worked. They hadn't intended to end up here; it just kind of happened. Being an administrative professional was not a point of pride, nor was it a source of shame. It just paid the bills.

For a while, I thought I was an anomaly. Where were the admins who loved the work? The ones who found it meaningful and important? The ones who wanted to excel in the role—not for the sake of getting away from it, but for the sake of being a *good* administrative partner.

Then, I discovered the internet. It was the mid-2000s, so this wasn't exactly a *new* discovery; I had been "surfing the web" for a few years. But I finally decided to tap into its power. Social media wasn't what it is today, so I started a blog for executive assistants called EA Toolbox.

That blog was both a public love letter to the administrative field and a desperate cry for camaraderie. I wanted to share everything I knew about being an assistant, little as that was at the time. But I also wanted to share my struggles and challenges, so others could chime in, commiserate, and offer their own advice.

I wrote blog post after blog post—and almost immediately, I found my people. In fact, I discovered a robust, global community of proud administrative professionals—career-minded individuals who appreciated and respected the admin field. I felt a profound sense of belonging unlike anything I had experienced before.

A funny thing happens when you write articles on the internet: People immediately believe you have some level of authority. As my blog became more and more popular, I became more "known" as a leader in the administrative field. I was quoted in the *Wall Street Journal*. My articles appeared on the websites of *Forbes*, Career Builder, and *U.S. News & World Report*. Admins were asking me to coach them and train their teams. I even wrote my first e-book, *The Effective Executive Assistant*.

There was a lot going on. I was a full-time EA running a booming side business. This hadn't been my plan.

And then, in February 2008, everything changed.

I was approached by an executive at a startup tech company. They were building a new online community for administrative professionals and wanted to talk to me about a possible partnership. About a month later, that company purchased my blog—something I didn't even know was possible—and hired me to be the Managing Editor and Community Spokesperson for the new website.

Obviously, this was a major turning point in my career and one I didn't take lightly. I made the decision to leave the admin field, but with the understanding that my new path would allow me to continue supporting those in the field. My new role gave me the opportunity to connect to an even larger admin network; it taught me the craft of presenting to large groups, and it gave me the confidence to truly embrace my position as a leader in the community.

Sadly, the startup company struggled and eventually folded. But by then, I had already felt called to start my own coaching and training business. That was in 2009, and today, business is better than it's ever been.

I realize my career path has been a little non-traditional, but everything evolved organically. I always felt as if I was taking the next natural step.

Admittedly, I've experienced many doubts along the way. For years, I was plagued by imposter syndrome. I was barely thirty years old when I started coaching and training. I didn't have decades of admin experience under my belt. Who was I to be teaching anything to anyone?

Thankfully, some of my earliest friends in the field, including Lisa Olsen (of Admin to Admin) and Julie Perrine (of All Things Admin), convinced me I did, indeed, have something valuable to share. They believed in me when I didn't always believe in myself. If not for them, I might have given up. To this day, they remain two of my most faithful and trusted supporters.

Slowly over the years, I've obtained the education and experience I need to feel comfortable being called a "career expert." While my business now serves a wide range of professionals, I still feel most at home with my administrative colleagues. I've trained admins within (literally) hundreds of organizations around the world, and each time, they teach me as much as I teach them. I now consider my collective experience with this diverse group of admins more valuable than my own personal experience in the role.

Today, I offer professional development training and resources through my website, EatYourCareer.com. That name is odd, I know, but the idea behind it is simple: I believe work can (and should) be a *nourishing*, enriching life experience. Creating that kind of career requires continuous learning—and that's what I'm here for.

To support this mission, I offer free monthly training webinars and Q&A sessions. I would love for you to join us! Sign up to get notified of upcoming sessions by visiting EatYourCareer.com/signup.

Much has changed in the last decade since I went into business for myself. In just the past few years especially, I have been amazed at the evolution that has taken place within the admin field. The community has experienced a renaissance of sorts—a reawakening of enthusiasm and renewal of spirit. Businesses are beginning to recognize both the power of the admin community and the untapped potential within it. Many are now investing considerable financial resources into the development of their admin teams. (This highly desirable benefit was, up until recently, only bestowed on leadership-level employees.)

With more attention being paid to the admin field, and more dollars flowing in, a wealth of new resources have become available. Today, admin conferences are regularly held in nearly every country in the world. We have been blessed with an abundance of books and online courses designed to educate, motivate, and empower the next generation of admins. Dozens of professional speakers, trainers, and authors now consider admins an important and lucrative target market, and each day, new "experts" pop up, eager to share their "Top Tips for Admin Success."

I believe all of this is a good thing for the admin community. I don't always agree with the perspectives shared by other admin influencers, but that's the point, isn't it? We all have a different take on things, and you may relate more to some of us than others, but we all share a passion for the profession.

For so long, admins were ignored and given little access to learning and development opportunities. There are still millions upon millions of admins who have no idea these resources exist! While admin-focused learning and development has certainly broken into the mainstream, it has, by no means, become the norm. The robust global community we have built still only represents a small fraction of the total admin population.

So, the more people we have out there serving and supporting admins, the better.

Of course, more voices bring more clutter. I do not want this book to just be noise in the background of an already crowded arena. My goal is to offer something different and substantial. Something unlike anything else you've seen or heard.

That's a high bar. Hold me to it.

This book is my *manifesto*, for lack of a better word.

That sounds scary, I know. Most people see that word and immediately think of some long-winded, self-indulgent, Unabomber-style rant.

This is not *that*.

In fact, let's wipe out all existing notions about that word and just look at the dictionary definition according to Merriam Webster:

> *Manifesto: A written statement declaring publicly the intentions, motives, or views of its issuer*

There's nothing inherently menacing in that definition. Manifestos don't have to be painfully long or nonsensical.

In fact, I promise you this: It won't feel like you're reading a manifesto. Instead, it will feel like we're having a conversation, you and me, about something that really matters. Participants in my training sessions use one word above all others to describe me: relatable. I hope you feel that as you read this book.

Imperfect as the word *manifesto* may be, I can think of no better word to describe this book. It is, indeed, my public declaration of so many things—my vision, beliefs, and perspective on all aspects of the administrative field.

Why should *you* care? Good question.

My intention in sharing these things is to help you build a vivid and enticing image of what's possible—not only for you as an administrative professional, but for the entire admin community.

My goal is to present you with ideas—a lot of them. Some will be massive and perhaps even outlandish; I hope you will find them interesting and inspiring to contemplate. Others will be simple and straightforward, tactical advice you can implement today.

Everything here is an offering. You are free to take what you like, adapt what you see fit, and leave the rest. I won't be offended. But please know that *everything* I offer comes from a place of deep love for this work. My desire is to help you create a thriving, fulfilling career as an administrative professional.

I want to pause here and define more specifically who exactly I'm speaking about when I say, "administrative professionals." I use this terminology because it is purposefully broad. I want to be as inclusive as possible in my discussion of this field.

Essentially, the "admins" I'm referring to encompass anyone whose primary job it is to provide support to someone or something (be it a single person, a group of people, or a business function) by handling the administrative work required to make that person or thing successful. I am referring to office professionals, not personal assistants working for families or celebrities (though surely many of the same strategies apply).

I recognize this definition covers a wide range of professionals with varying levels of responsibility and expertise. So, let me narrow this down a bit more.

I imagine there are 3 different kinds of people who may find themselves reading this book:

1. **Administrative professionals who have already reached the top levels of the field, namely C-Suite Executive Assistants.** It is my presumption that those of you in this category are seeking a deeper, more nuanced discussion of the field in which you operate. You may be looking for opportunities to enrich your own experience in the workplace as well as strategies to help develop and mentor up-and-coming admins. This book will honor your knowledge and expertise, and at the same time, challenge you to think differently in some critically important ways.

2. **Enthusiastic admins who are early to mid-career and striving to excel in the role.** To those of you in this category: You're in the right place. Whatever spark of excitement you have now, prepare for it to catch fire as you read. This book will help you see the opportunities before you—but remember that growth only happens when knowledge meets action. I encourage you to focus on implementation.

3. **Leaders who are looking to better understand and, indeed,** *elevate* **their administrative team.** Whether you're a Human Resources (HR) professional, an executive, or any other type of organizational leader, let me extend a special welcome to you. Obviously, you already appreciate the role of support staff and are willing to invest your own time, energy, and attention into their development. You play a very important part in this story. This book will potentially forever change the way you see your administrative team. The choices you make with this new perspective may have the power to dramatically impact your organization and the people within it.

Throughout this book, however, I am primarily speaking directly to my administrative friends. This is to whom I am referring when I use the word "you," or occasionally, "we." When discussing the people admins support, I generally call them "executives" or "leaders." You are welcome to mentally replace these words if they do not reflect the terms to which you are accustomed.

The word "admin" itself can cause some confusion, especially for those who are not already fluent in the language of this field. As is common, I may use "admin" to describe an individual (i.e., *she is an admin*) and to describe a collective group (i.e., *the admin field*). That being said, I often prefer the more formal terminology, "administrative professional" or the more inclusive option, "support professional."

Sadly, there's a whole category of people who will likely never see this book, though they probably have the most to gain from it. I'm referring to administrative professionals who do not value the position—the ones I briefly mentioned earlier, who consider it a "dead end" job or think the work is beneath them. These are the people who really *need* this information. They are out there, in great numbers. Though their attitude is typically a byproduct of ignorance, it's detrimental for them and for us. When you encounter them, please share what you learn here. Help them understand there is another perspective, and it's a vastly more rewarding one.

I do, of course, have my own share of limitations. I do not claim to be the ultimate authority in the field; I am merely one voice. Recognize that I am speaking from a U.S.-based perspective and my own personal experience. Where it makes sense, I cite the wisdom of others and provide well-documented, reliable data to support my views. I also cite the experiences of others, where appropriate, as I find stories are often the most effective learning tools. In most cases, I've changed the names of individuals to protect their privacy. Where I share both a first and last name, the individual has provided me with permission to share their story.

Finally, you should know that "ELEVATE Admins" is also the name I use for my certificate program for administrative professionals and teams. Until 2020, this program was only offered as an in-person program for organizations. However, with the increasing popularity of online training, I now offer it in a virtual format publicly once a year. This book does *not* cover the same content found in the course curriculum, though it is aligned in overall concept and tone. You might consider this book "Level Zero" for the program or a prerequisite. If you like what you read here and are interested in obtaining deeper training, please visit www.ElevateAdmins.com to learn more. There, you will also find some supplemental materials to help you get even more out of this book.

Now that I've explained what we're doing here and where we're going, let's dive into the wonderful world of admin together!

2

THE EVOLVING ADMIN

I like to say admin work is "in my blood" because my mother was a career secretary. In fact, she's the one who inspired my *Secretary* game. I remember, as a child, visiting the law office where she worked and watching her interact with clients and colleagues. It all seemed so glamorous to my young eyes!

My mother retired many years ago now, but she keeps up with trends in the field through me. Together, we often marvel at the incredible evolution that's taken place.

I ended my employment as an admin in 2008, which doesn't seem that long ago. But in the modern working world, a lifetime has passed. Heck, when I was an EA, we still used fax machines—*daily*—and Blackberries were all the rage. (I still miss that tiny little keyboard!)

Technology isn't all that's changed; it's just the most obvious element. The equipment and tools of the modern admin resemble little of those used even a decade or two ago. But beneath the surface, shifting social and cultural dynamics have had an equally (and perhaps even *more*) powerful impact on the evolution of the role.

In biology, evolution is the term used to describe how a species adapts over generations through a process of natural selection. It is a requirement for any species to survive over time. Admins are no exception. Through the years, we've evolved based on a number of different factors, and this evolution has allowed us to remain a viable, valuable part of the business community.

It is, therefore, only natural to presume that our continued existence will rely on further evolution. What does that look like? I have some ideas. No one can predict the future, but there are some pretty clear trends that, I believe, point us in an obvious direction.

But I'm getting ahead of myself. Evolution is not an overnight process; it's a gradual series of micro-changes that are often only appreciated in hindsight.

Understanding the Past

To understand where the admin field is and where it is going, we must start by exploring where it's been. History provides important context.

The admin profession was born out of the secretarial field.

A lot of people don't like the word "secretary." In fact, some folks downright despise it. As a title, it's become much less common in the U.S., though globally, it doesn't seem to carry the same negative connotations.

I personally don't mind the word, primarily because it reminds me of my mother, and she's pretty amazing. But I also don't believe there's any shame in secretarial work. The outdated stigma of the title is based largely on a distorted view of what the role was in the past.

In truth, secretaries have always held very important, though understated, positions. The word itself was derived from the Latin word for *secret*. Inherent in the title of "secretary" is the understanding that this person is a trusted keeper of confidential information. It's no surprise that the title is still used for many top-ranking government roles, such as Secretary of State in the U.S.

In the 1800s, secretarial roles were entry-level business positions largely held by men. However, by the 1920s, women dominated the field. According to a 2006 article in the *Chicago Tribune* ("A job once filled by men became a pink profession" by Amy Eagle), this change was due to a number of contributing factors, including but not limited to:

- **The invention and mass production of the typewriter.** Odd as it sounds, women were believed to have more nimble, thinner fingers which were considered better for operating new-fangled office machinery.
- **Increased access to free public high school.** This

meant a greater number of young women were educated. Plus, girls' curriculum would often include typing while boys learned carpentry.

- **Booming business after the Civil War and the Industrial Revolution.** Office workers were in high demand, but industrial jobs, like construction and mining, were also plentiful. Following traditional gender roles of the time, men gravitated to the latter, while women were drawn to the former.

With women making up the majority of the secretarial field, it eventually became synonymous with "women's work." This quickly gave way to stereotypes about the women who held these roles—that they were like homemakers for the office, den mothers for executive leaders, or even second wives for their counterparts. The secretary's job was dumbed down in the public eye. Soon, it was presumed to be little more than making coffee and straightening the boss's tie.

This image of the pretty but vapid, professionally inconsequential secretary was, of course, ridiculous. It was a *sexist caricature*—an exaggerated, insulting misrepresentation of the role.

Being a secretary was (and is) a good, honorable job. Up until the 1960s or so, it was one of few employment options for women who didn't have a college degree. It gave many women, including my mother, an opportunity to have a career and financially support their families.

Admittedly, the job then was not what it is now. But it was important, nonetheless. As with modern day admins, some secretaries had greater responsibilities than others. Some took it more seriously than others and some were more skilled. Regardless, they all deserved respect, though many did not receive it.

Perhaps the lack of respect toward secretaries of the past contributed to what eventually became known as the Women's Liberation Movement. Aimed at helping women achieve social and economic equality and independence, this movement started in the late 1960s and continued into the 1980s. Working women were at the forefront, pushing for better pay, more opportunities, and more R-E-S-P-E-C-T.

In 1980, the movie *9 to 5* reflected the overall sentiment at the time. A hilarious parody, the movie depicts three secretaries who are perpetually mistreated by their "sexist, egotistical, lying, hypocritical bigot" boss. Through a series of outrageous events, the women end up kidnapping the boss and holding him hostage. Meanwhile at the office, the women initiate a wide variety of well-received employee-friendly changes like flexible work hours, equal pay for men and women, and a job-sharing program. In the boss's absence, they are finally able to let their intelligence shine for all to see.

We owe a lot to the feminists of the past, many of whom were secretaries. Today, the administrative field is still 95 percent female, and we're still slowly chipping away at *some* of the old stigmas. But much of the most egregiously sexist attitudes and actions of the past are now deemed inappropriate (or illegal) in the modern workplace.

Throughout the '80s and '90s, the secretarial role evolved dramatically. This largely coincided with the increasing access to computers and other office technology. Administrative work was suddenly given an upgrade. Some of the more menial tasks, like directing calls and filing paperwork, became nearly obsolete and were replaced with new, more sophisticated tasks like electronic calendaring, email management, word processing, and more.

The title of *secretary* no longer seemed to fit the new job description, and thus, a new name was born. Well, *many* new names. Different organizations began using different titles, a fact that has created a lot of confusion still today. Assistant, coordinator, administrator—there are literally hundreds of titles that fall under the broad umbrella of being "administrative" in nature. At some point, "administrative professional" became the overarching, catch-all title embraced by the community.

In 2000, National Secretaries Day (originally created by the National Secretaries Association in 1952) was officially changed to Administrative Professionals Week and its creator is now known as the International Association for Administrative Professionals. This change marked a major milestone in the evolution of the field.

Exploring the Present

While the community has adopted the informal "administrative professional" moniker, there has still been no formal, standard naming convention embraced across the board inside organizations. This presents a number of different problems, particularly with regard to varying performance standards in the field and tracking employment data (which I'll touch on more later).

To be clear, secretaries still do exist. However, in the U.S., the title is often considered most appropriate for receptionist-level positions. Some organizations, especially those with a global workforce, still use the secretary title even for higher level administrative roles, but the trend continues to be moving away from it.

Today, *administrative assistant* and *executive assistant* tend to be the most popular titles in the field. Generally speaking, the former indicates a lower level of responsibility and a one-to-many relationship, where the assistant supports a group of people, a department, or a business function. The latter usually indicates a higher level of responsibility and a one-to-few or even one-to-one partnership between a senior leader and administrative staff member.

As mentioned previously, I believe the administrative field, which encompasses all of these roles, is in the midst of a very exciting renaissance. However, there are some factors that (on the surface) don't necessarily support this view, so let me address those first.

According to the U.S. Bureau of Labor Statistics, the admin field is shrinking. In fact, the data suggests that, since the year 2000, "secretarial and administrative assistant" positions have declined by as much as 40 percent and overall employment in the field is projected to decline 9 percent from 2019 to 2029.

Before you panic, let me offer this important caveat: the data we have is not, necessarily, adequate to paint a complete picture.

At the time of this writing, the U.S. Department of Labor (DOL) lumps a lot of titles together in the "secretarial and administrative assistant" group. It includes everything from receptionists and personal assistants to executive-level support staff and roles that require specific expertise (such as legal and medical assistants).

Additionally, due to the wide variety of titles that exist in the marketplace, it's likely that some groups have been missed entirely. Advocates for the profession are currently working to encourage the DOL to create separate categories that will more accurately capture the full breadth and depth of the field and distinguish the lower- or entry-level roles from the higher-level, more expertise-driven roles.

Until that happens, we'll have to settle for the data we have, which indicates the field is shrinking. I prefer a different term —*advancing*.

Based on my experience and common sense, I think it's reasonable to believe that the administrative field, as a whole, is declining in numbers. This is particularly true for the more generic and lower-level administrative roles. Technology has taken over many of the common admin tasks of the past, or at least made them dramatically more efficient. We don't need an entire group of people sitting at a switchboard transferring calls. Most executives don't need someone to take dictation anymore, because they're perfectly comfortable typing up their own correspondence on the computer. Consequently, each individual admin is able to do much more with his or her time and support more people at once.

I believe this present-day evolution means there is more opportunity than ever for those who remain in the field. As the straightforward work is delegated to computers, it leaves those in administrative roles more time and brain power to focus on the big stuff—things that have a real impact on the business, such as process improvement, problem-solving, project management, and relationship building. The more technology gets involved, the more availability admins have to be used as true business partners, rather than task runners.

This change has put a greater emphasis on *skill*. Administrative professionals are now handling much more in terms of volume, and also in terms of responsibility. Their duties are more sophisticated and require a higher level of business acumen. This explains the increased focus in recent years on training and development for the field, as well as the increased number of administrative professionals who hold college degrees.

The Impact of COVID-19

In 2020, as a result of the global pandemic, the administrative field experienced several *years* of evolution in a matter of mere months.

Until this point, it was a common belief that administrative professionals needed to be physically present in the office to function properly. Remote positions were few and far between in the traditional corporate employee world. Virtual assistance was terminology reserved for professionals providing offsite support services independently to clients on a freelance or contract basis.

This all changed when large numbers of support professionals were forced to work from home for at least some period of time during the pandemic. Admins and the people they support had no choice but to quickly learn the necessary technology, tools, and processes to work productively from separate locations. And remarkably, most managed just fine. (Some surely were more successful than others, but the admin field did not collapse.)

This revelation—that admins can still support their leaders adequately from anywhere—represents an enormous shift in the field, and it's one that arguably provides a lot of benefits for both the executive and the admin. When hiring support staff, leaders are no longer limited to the local pool of candidates. Likewise, when seeking employment options, admins have a global marketplace to explore.

This, however, creates an even more competitive market. Additionally, due to the economic uncertainty caused by the pandemic, the number of support roles has been even further reduced. And, in the midst of the work-from-home experiment, some rather misguided leaders (left to their own devices) decided they didn't actually need their admins after all. Once their support staff was out of sight, they quickly became out of mind as well.

I believe strongly that high-functioning leaders *need* administrative support, and sooner or later, the ones who jumped to the erroneous conclusion that they don't will come back to their senses. However, it raises an important point for the future of the admin profession: For those working in remote positions, it is especially imperative to consistently demonstrate your value and maintain a high level of visibility. Today's leaders are highly self-sufficient, but admin work is still not the best and highest use of their time.

Still, there are plenty of administrative professionals and leaders who discovered in 2020 that virtual work is not for them. Many experienced feelings of deep isolation—a problem that had already plagued the admin community even before the pandemic. A lot of people realized they prefer the traditional office environment and want to be in the same physical space with their team. In fact, the forced separation made them appreciate these things more!

Therefore, I do not believe remote administrative support will become the new, permanent norm. It will certainly become more prevalent, and perhaps a hybrid or blended approach will become popular as well. Ultimately, this experience has expanded our collective understanding of what's possible.

Without question, however, virtual meeting and collaboration technology is here to stay. Even those who were most resistant were forced to get comfortable with it, and now that we all have, it is likely to permanently remain a heavily relied on fixture in our technological ecosystem.

The Administrative Field of the Future

When discussing the future, admins often get a little fearful. That's perfectly okay! In fact, you wouldn't be normal if you weren't at least a little concerned. Each day, we're bombarded by talk of imminent planetary disaster, while simultaneously being warned that robots and artificial intelligence (AI) are taking over. Fear seems a pretty natural response.

But there's always another side of the equation. As author Dee Wilson so poignantly said, "Fear is just excitement in need of an attitude adjustment."

As an administrative community, I believe our attitude about the future of our profession should be one of excitement, rather than fear. There is so much to look forward to.

Yes, the field is evolving, and it will continue to, perhaps even *more* rapidly in the future. Some pessimistic theorists suggest the future will see the end of the administrative field, but I think that's nonsense. It's not going anywhere, but it *is* going to be different.

I believe the role of administrative professionals in the future will possess three distinct characteristics: It will be collaborative, connected, and creative.

COLLABORATIVE

"Partnership" will become the key terminology to describe the relationship between administrative professionals and the person or people they support. This language has already gained popularity in the recent past, but the future will see "partner" grow into the default description and perhaps even the official title within organizations.

Several forward-thinking companies have already taken this approach. For example, at the time of this writing, Google and Pinterest both use "executive *business partner*" instead of executive assistant, and "administrative *business partner*" instead of administrative assistant.

This linguistic change might seem relatively inconsequential, but it places a deeper emphasis on the relationship and elevates the admin role from worker bee to trusted ally, at least optically for others.

While executives of the future will continue to grow more and more self-sufficient, they will also come to realize that administrative duties are neither their strong suit, nor a wise use of their time and attention. They will lean even more heavily on their administrative partners to manage these items and, at the same time, manage *them*.

As the demands placed on executives increase, they will need support professionals who can effectively "manage up" to help keep them on time, on task, and on target. They will expect their administrative partners to act as alter egos, anticipate needs, take initiative, and work autonomously.

This increased emphasis on relationships extends far beyond that of the partnership. While technology will, indeed, continue to make some administrative tasks unnecessary, and robots (AI) will undoubtedly take over others, there are certain uniquely human activities that computers will never be able to do. Compassion, empathy, and camaraderie are all important emotional needs that help create social bonds in the workplace —a requirement for effective teamwork. Admins have always played a critical (though intangible) role in developing the right atmosphere for group productivity, and this will become an even more vital aspect of the role in the future.

To a certain extent, we already saw this play out during the pandemic, as administrative professionals took the lead in helping keep newly dispersed teams engaged. Admins were the ones reaching out to their colleagues to ask, "How are you doing?" They organized virtual happy hours and trivia games.

They used every tool at their disposal to ensure everyone on the team had what they needed to not only continue working, but to maintain a spirit of togetherness in the midst of chaos.

CONNECTED

Not surprisingly, the global workplace of the future will be even more connected. With our increased comfort and reliance on virtual meeting and collaboration technology, administrative professionals will have a far greater reach and ability for impact.

They will, increasingly, provide virtual support to global executives—some of whom they may never meet in person. This will require exceptional self-management skills and the ability to work efficiently without direct supervision. Admins will also need to demonstrate awareness and appreciation of different cultures and an ability to communicate effectively without the benefit of physical presence.

As in the past, admins will continue to interact with people at all levels inside and outside of the organization. They will need to work cross-functionally and bring people together across physical, virtual, and even ideological boundaries. In doing so, they will need to demonstrate exceptional levels of diplomacy and negotiation skills, as well as masterful logistics management, coordinating people and resources across multiple time zones at once.

Increased connection also brings more opportunities for the global admin network. In the future, admins will be able to connect with *one another* like never before, which means a greater ability to leverage the wisdom of colleagues across the globe. Admins who feel isolated within their organizations will find a welcoming, all-inclusive community in the online world. Challenges that previously had to be managed by each individual will benefit from group problem-solving, leading to faster, better results. (We've already seen an example of this during the pandemic as admins flooded social media to share tips, particularly with regard to travel rearrangement.)

Additionally, the rise of remote work in the field brings even more opportunity for admins interested in self-employment. It's important to note that virtual assistance (VA) is not the same as working virtually in a traditional support role. However, many of the same skills apply. For those who thrive in the remote environment and are interested in business ownership, the VA sector is likely to continue booming in years to come.

CREATIVE

This last element may sound odd. After all, admins aren't artists. What does creativity have to do with it?

Quite a bit, actually.

Thanks to technology, the admin role will become less task-driven and, therefore, less oriented toward systems and procedures. You can easily define a step-by-step process for tackling a task, but higher-level, more complicated work requires creativity—the ability to think abstractly and come up with new approaches. The emphasis will be not on the task at hand, but on the result, and the admin will have flexibility in how the result is reached.

This means admins will have to get comfortable with experimentation—something that has not, historically, been required or encouraged in this role. The workplace of the future, however, will reward those who are willing and able to take intelligent risks.

Once again, we saw examples of this during the pandemic. In many cases, admins were told to operate from home, without any existing roadmap in place. They had to build entirely new policies and procedures from scratch not only for themselves, but often for their teams and leaders as well.

This ability to adapt on-the-fly and keep things running while simultaneously creating something new will become a hallmark of the administrative role.

Shifting Perceptions: The Work Continues

I also believe that in the future, it will be our responsibility, as an administrative community, to follow in the footsteps of our predecessors and continue to help shift perceptions of the role. The stigma of the past haunts us in many ways. Admins still frequently feel their work is discounted and not respected by others. They still see themselves as invisible superheroes, making magic behind a curtain without ever receiving the recognition or appreciation they deserve.

Note: These topics are explored more deeply in chapter 9, and even more extensively in my book, The Invisibility Cure: How to Stand Out, Get Noticed and Get What You Want at Work, *available on Amazon.*

One of the most common refrains I hear from admins is this: "People have no idea what I do all day!" Herein lies the problem. The admin role is still a mystery to many people. From the outside looking in, *any* job can appear easier than it is.

If people don't know what you do, educate them. Help them understand the value of your work. Explain how you make that magic of yours—the time and skill it requires. If people have inaccurate ideas about your role, correct them.

Above all, do not contribute to negative or inaccurate perceptions by discounting your own work. Never—and I mean *never*—refer to yourself as "just" an admin. That tiny little word has plagued our field for generations. It means something very specific in the English language. When you say "just," it is like a linguistic red flag signaling that whatever comes next is not important. You are not *just* anything.

You're a valuable and proud administrative partner. Let that belief permeate your thoughts, actions, and words. Realize that there are likely people within your organization who would do anything to get five minutes with the leaders you support all day long. They lose sleep thinking about talking to these leaders; meanwhile, you are developing productive *relationships* with them. You are guiding them, influencing them, and partnering with them.

You are both fortunate and powerful in your position.

Changing perceptions is not an overnight proposition. It's like turning a huge ship—a slow and steady process. But we are the ones steering the ship. No one else is going to do it for us.

My Hopes for the Future

As a trainer who specializes in working with administrative teams, I often find myself very busy presenting at multiple organizations throughout the month of April.

You see, Administrative Professional's Day, which is traditionally the last Wednesday of April, slowly became Admin Week, and now it's become Admin Month. During this time, many organizations host development activities and appreciation events. Some executives even make it a practice to provide their staff with gifts—like flowers or candy.

I believe, wholeheartedly, that this is a lovely concept.

But I also have a desperate desire to see it disappear. I would love nothing more.

Why? Well, consider this: What other professions have a special day of appreciation? There are a few; teachers and nurses tend to be the most commonly cited when I ask this question in training classes. And what do these roles have in common with admins? They are all traditionally female-dominated fields and they all have a reputation for being underappreciated.

It is my wish that one day in the future, admins won't need a special day, week, or month of appreciation, because they will be recognized and acknowledged for their valuable contributions every day of the year. I don't believe flowers and candy, or even training opportunities, offered during one special month are sufficient.

My hope is that the administrative profession will continue to advance in years to come and gain the respect it deserves. I believe it's possible, and you should, too. It truly does start with us.

3

JOB VS. CAREER

I n each of the earlier chapters, I implied a distinction between administrative professionals who think of their work as a job versus those who see it as a career.

This is a useful topic to explore in depth because there's often a good deal of confusion around these two words. But beyond that, I believe language is powerful. The words we use to describe ourselves and our work can impact not only how others view us, but how we view ourselves. Therefore, it's important to understand how exactly a job differs from a career —and, if you really want this to be your career, what is required of you.

The Difference Between a Job and a Career

While there are a lot of different approaches to this topic, I think of it like this: A job is an activity in exchange for payment.

A career is the pursuit of an ambition or progression toward a goal.

Ideally, you want your job to be aligned with your career, meaning that any job you have moves you forward (in some way) on your path toward achieving your ambitions or goals.

So, if you're a career administrative professional, you may currently be working in a job as an executive assistant to the VP of Marketing. You could change jobs and go to another organization, but as long as you're still in the field of admin, you haven't changed careers.

On the other hand, if you're an aspiring chef and you're working as an admin at your local real estate office, you have a job—but it's not really a career. It's just a way of making ends meet while you get your foot in the door elsewhere.

It makes sense that these two individuals would approach work with entirely different mindsets. Neither one is "right" or "wrong." However, the second individual (the chef), has a greater potential for dissatisfaction. Working a job that doesn't align with your career ambitions can be frustrating and soulless. Yet, for some people, it's an unavoidable reality.

Still, there is another kind of person—the one who *appears* to have a career, but still treats their work as "just a job." This happens frequently in the administrative field. I've met people who have worked in the field for *decades* and yet, they still do not claim to have a career. Instead, they consider it a series of jobs.

I believe having a career is inherently satisfying, but it's as much mental as it is physical. *Looking* as if you have a career on the outside, but not *feeling* it on the inside, puts you in the same lousy spot as the aspiring chef who is working an admin job. You're probably not going to get a lot of fulfillment from your situation.

Some people think that, to be a career, the work has to meet some standard of difficulty or require an exceptional level of education. For this reason, many admins (especially those newer to the field) will automatically count themselves out.

There are no such requirements for something to be considered a career. Administrative professionals can make this work their career if they so choose.

Having a career is really about making a commitment. Simply thinking of your work as a career can positively impact your feelings about it. And, for better or worse, how you feel about your work will come out in your behaviors, which will ultimately impact your results.

The table in Figure 1 provides some key differentiators between the "just a job" mindset and the career mindset. Review the items listed and evaluate your current state of mind.

"JUST A JOB" MINDSET	CAREER MINDSET
Short-term approach	Long-term approach
Money is the primary motivator	Experience and growth are the primary motivators
The job description is the highest expectation; if it's not there, it's not happening	The job description is the minimum expectation; you're willing to go above and beyond
Flying under the radar	Raising visibility
Complacency and stagnancy	Continuous growth and learning
Sporadic, minimal achievement	Consistent progress and achievement
Takes a passive role in defining direction	Takes an active role in defining direction
Expects organization to provide learning opportunities; unwilling to invest personally	Takes responsibility for identifying and pursuing learning opportunities; willing to invest personally if needed

Figure 1. Job vs. Career Mindset Comparison

It's okay if admin is just a job to you, though I presume few people reading this book think of it that way. If you do, I hope you have another career you're aspiring to and working toward in your off-hours.

It's also okay if admin is a stepping stone for you—if your goal is to leverage the experience you gain here in another field in the future. Taking the career mindset now, even at this stage, will certainly serve you well.

My primary concern is for those who want a career, but are still thinking and acting like they're in a job. All too often, people want the rewards of a career (fulfillment, growth, etc.), while putting in the effort of a job.

If admin isn't necessarily the career you *want*, but (on paper) it's the career you've got, then you have some options:

- You can disown it as a career, treat it as a job forever, and accept the inevitable consequences of that.
- You can go find yourself a different job in the career you want.
- You can embrace what is and make this your *career of choice*.

Let's dive deeper into that last concept.

Career of Choice vs. Default Career

There's a distinction I want to make here, and it may appear as if I'm splitting hairs, but this is an important point. Choosing your career path is different from simply landing in a career by default.

Let me explain. When I ask administrative professionals how they got started in the field, a lot of them respond by saying some version of this: "I just kind of fell into it…"

Most of these people are career admins, but with this phrasing, they're abdicating responsibility for it.

To be clear, the words may, indeed, be accurate. I know many admins do not intentionally set out to make this a career. But this kind of language makes the person sound like a victim. It's as if they're saying, "I was trapped! I was tricked! I didn't sign up for this, and now I'm stuck here!"

"Falling" into a career suggests it wasn't a choice. It only became a career for these folks because they never chose anything different.

This whole concept comes from a disempowered, passive place. Having a career by default suggests you're not in control of your own destiny; you're just riding the stream of life wherever it happens to take you.

The truth is, sometimes you pick the path, and sometimes the path picks you.

But once you're on the path—once admin is, indeed, your career —it's time to embrace it. *Choose* it, even in retrospect. Make a conscious decision to be a career administrative professional and take ownership of that choice.

How did you get started in this field? Call it a happy accident. You were drawn to some aspect of your first job in admin, and you discovered it suited you. You progressively grew and built a career you're proud of.

You didn't fall. You took a leap of faith and this is where you landed.

Though the difference may seem subtle, it can have a dramatic impact on your mindset.

How you think about yourself and the path you're on can influence everything about your self-presentation—how you carry yourself around the office, the tone with which you speak about your role, the confidence you have when interacting with colleagues. All of these things can and will affect how others see you and the opportunities they afford you in the future.

When Does a Career Become a Calling?

Just as a job can become a career, a career can become a calling.

Here again is another frequently misunderstood word.

Many people think a calling requires some kind of profound spiritual experience, like hearing a voice from the heavens explaining your life's mission.

Others believe having "a calling" means you're a natural—the work comes easy—or it means you experience an immediate, overwhelming sense of joy when engaging in it.

All of these ideas are false, though they each have an inkling of truth.

Yes, a calling involves work you feel passionately about. But that doesn't mean every minute of the day will be filled with joy. That's just unrealistic.

Yes, a calling involves work you're good at, but that doesn't mean it's easy. You may have to work hard to learn the skills required to become good—and that process is, itself, rewarding. It actually adds to the fulfillment of the endeavor.

And yes, a calling is a somewhat spiritual experience, but it's not as blatant as a heavenly voice directing you. When your work is a calling, it gives you a sense of connection and purpose. It aligns with your values and character. It feels *right*.

Even when your work is a calling, it's still work. There are still aspects that drive you crazy, and you still have bad days like the rest of us. Don't set yourself up for disappointment by believing there is some magical level of career bliss that will change all that.

I have encountered many people who feel admin is, indeed, their calling. I asked a woman recently to elaborate on her feelings. She said her calling is to help and support others, and she gets to do that through her role as an administrative professional.

This is, perhaps, the ultimate state-of-mind around work—the feeling that you *get* to do something—that it's a privilege.

Any career can become a calling with the right mindset. By approaching work with an open mind and open heart, you can begin to see the incredible alignment of the universe that brought you to this place.

The Art of Job Shaping or Career Crafting

Even those who have successfully made admin their career of choice may occasionally find themselves in a role that doesn't fit their skillset perfectly or in a position that leaves them wanting something different or something more. Admin roles can vary dramatically from one organization to another; different leaders want different support. Sometimes a job is "sold" as one thing, but the reality just doesn't match.

This kind of situation can make you question your own abilities and your career choices. But fear not! There are almost always a number of things you can do to make an imperfect job a little closer to perfect. This process is commonly referred to as "job shaping" or "career crafting."

These terms describe the process of redesigning and renegotiating the elements of your role to better suit your individual wants and needs. It's about defining your goals and carving a path to make them happen.

You can use this strategy in a variety of situations to help mold your career into what you want it to be.

I believe administrative roles have a lot of potential for this. However, it takes effort on your part. This is an employee-initiated career development process, which means it's your responsibility. Don't expect your boss to suggest it; you must advocate for yourself.

For those with a career mindset, this process provides a lot of benefits. It allows you to grow professionally and achieve that sense of fulfillment and engagement you're looking for—without having to find a new job. Most career admins want to stay in any given job for *at least* two to five years and experience professional growth during that time. Most also consider job searching a stressful, time-consuming process, and (no matter how discerning you are) you can never guarantee the next job will be any better than your last. So, why not attempt to mold what you currently have into something that feels better aligned?

This process is also beneficial for your organization. If you're happier with your role, you're likely to stick around longer and perform at higher levels while you're there.

Of course, there are limitations. Within any role, there are always non-negotiable elements. You can't expect to rework every piece of your job. Your organization hired you to do certain things, and while some adjustments may be possible (within the confines of your current role), others won't (without an actual change in job).

Further, timing is a very important part of this process. You need to wait until you really know the role and the organizational/team culture. Never attempt to redesign your role immediately after being hired. This will indicate that you didn't accept the job in good faith, and it may damage your reputation.

Lastly, to successfully practice job shaping or career crafting, you need supportive and relatively flexible leadership. The person or people you support must value your development and want to see you succeed, even if that means reallocating some elements of the work to accommodate your career needs and wants. Ideally, your leaders will care more about retaining you (a great employee) and keeping you happy than they will care about "boxing" you in to your existing job description.

To successfully redesign your role, you must first have enough self-awareness to know the aspects of the role that are not a match for your skills and career interests, and what you would like to focus on instead. Perhaps this book will help you better identify these things!

Once you have clarity, discuss your career goals and preferences with your immediate supervisor and ask for support. Define specifically what you'd like to do more of (e.g., contribute to a certain type of project, coach admins who are new to the team, or get more deeply involved in corporate governance) and what you'd like to do less of (e.g., managing expense reports, taking meeting minutes, or planning travel).

Needless to say, these kinds of requests go over best for people who have a proven track record of exceptional performance, and for those who already have ideas about how to make these changes happen. For example, perhaps you can automate or streamline some of those less desirable tasks to help reduce your focus on them. Or maybe you can identify another admin who wants more experience with these items to whom you can delegate or reallocate the work. Presenting a well-thought-out plan of action will always improve your chances of success.

Later, in chapter 7, I'll share the inspiring story of Michelle, a former coaching client of mine who not only reshaped her role, but carved out an entirely new career path for herself in the process.

In my experience, many leaders are open to this idea, but they also understand it can be a challenge. Part of your job is to make it as easy on them as possible. One way you can do that is to take it slow! Don't try to dramatically reshape your role over the span of a few days or even weeks. Realize that changes within your job territory can have a ripple impact, and it can take time to figure out how to make it work for everyone.

The Importance of Ongoing Learning

One of the primary things that distinguishes a person who views work as a job versus one who sees it as a career or even a calling is a demonstrated desire to learn. By obtaining education, certification, and/or training in your field, you exhibit unmistakable commitment. After all, these things take time, energy, and money. When you voluntarily invest these valuable, limited resources toward the pursuit of deepening your professional expertise, you show the world that you take your work seriously.

Admin is an interesting field in that is does not necessarily *require* a degree for entry, growth, or reaching exceptionally high levels of success. However, some organizations may require a degree, just as some specialized roles might (like legal or medical assistants). I certainly do not discount the value of higher education, but by and large, administrative professionals have traditionally tended to rely more on a combination of hands-on experience and field-specific (non-collegiate) learning.

Still, I frequently hear from administrative professionals, including those at the highest levels, who worry that they should go back to school to get a degree. Though they realize it may not be an essential component for their career path, they have a little self-sabotaging voice that says, "You're not good enough," simply because they lack this level of formal education.

In my experience, not having a college degree is often more important to the person who lacks it than to anyone else. In the modern working world, a certain level of experience is usually considered commensurate with (or equal to) a degree— especially in the administrative field.

Most leaders today recognize that college is not financially feasible for everyone, and many view real-world experience as the best education there is. In many organizations, the degree you have or don't have is of minor consequence. (This is not true for all, of course, but it's more common than you might realize.)

That being said, some industries and organizations *do* require a degree for administrative roles, particularly higher-level ones (such as executive assistant, chief of staff, administrative manager, etc.). Without one, you will eventually reach a ceiling. If that describes an industry or organization you want to be a part of, you're better off finding a way to go get that degree.

Sure, you can try to fight the system and, in rare cases, you may be successful. But there's no guarantee. Obviously, there's a reason the degree has become such a crucial qualification for the work you want to do. It either provides some element of education you simply can't learn efficiently or effectively on-the-job, or it's seen as a valuable tradition that people are not willing to do away with. In either case, it's unlikely anything else will compensate for a missing degree, so it may well be worth your time and financial investment to obtain it. Only you can make that decision.

If not having your degree is weighing heavily on your self-esteem or if you simply want to have the experience of higher education, I personally believe there's never any drawback to learning. The only downside is the financial requirement to obtain it, so do your research and take advantage of every kind of aid possible.

In Defense of Higher Education

While I stand by my belief that a college degree is not *necessary* in the administrative world, I recently had a conversation that helped me appreciate the importance of higher education in the field nonetheless. Laura Kaufman is an experienced executive assistant and educator, and an advocate for higher education, particularly within the admin community. In our recent meeting, Laura brought up some excellent points, and I want to share a few of them with you here.

- **There is a distinction between training and education.** Training teaches you how to do things, while education teaches you to think critically about problems and figure out the solutions yourself. Training is more focused on step-by-step instruction and developing your marketable job skills based on the present needs of the field, which can still be beneficial. But education is about developing *yourself* to make *you* a more marketable professional. Therefore, it stands to reason that education is a more long-term career investment.

- **A degree can open doors**. More and more, companies are seeking administrative professionals with college degrees. In fact, according to a *Wall Street Journal* article published in 2020 ("The Vanishing Executive Assistant" by Rachel Feintzeig), the percentage of admins who hold a bachelor's degree or higher has been steadily increasing since 2000. Consequently, those who do not possess one are likely competing with those who do. All things being equal, the degree can certainly be an added selling point. It's also not unusual to find roles that combine admin with other job duties, such as business analysis, which may make a degree even more desirable. It can be especially beneficial for those who are seeking to advance to higher levels either within the admin field or outside of it.

- **There are options that make obtaining higher education easier for working people**. Some degree programs will award credit for work experience or even field-specific certification. It takes effort to understand how it all works and provide the supporting documentation, but it may reduce the time and financial investment.

- **Consider the return on investment**. Conferences often cost two or three thousand dollars (including travel and hotel expenses), while a community college class can cost just a few hundred. When weighing the options, ask yourself, "Which will have the greatest potential for a strong return?" Conferences may be more immediately gratifying, and perhaps more fun, but it may be worth it to put them off for a few years in exchange for earning your degree.

Laura Kaufman is a career admin, currently working as a C-Suite executive assistant. She obtained her bachelor's degree while working full time and raising four kids as a single mother. Now a mother of six, she is also an adjunct instructor at College of Lake County and, in spring 2021, she enrolled in Northwestern University's Professional Studies program, focusing on project management.

There are many forms of education in this world. In some cases, a current, reputable professional certification may actually be more relevant and valuable than a college degree. Why? Because a college degree is a form of stagnant education. It doesn't evolve. You get it and you're done. You have a degree.

On the other hand, to maintain a professional certification you often have to engage in continuing education. You have to keep your skills up-to-date to keep that certification valid. So, your education is continuously evolving with your field.

I'll give you a quick example: I earned my bachelor's degree in business administration & marketing in 2001. That was before social media was even a thing. Consequently, my marketing degree is actually pretty irrelevant in the modern world, because I never did any course work that had to do with today's most powerful marketing tool—the internet. If I were trying to work in the marketing field, I would want to supplement my degree with a current professional certification to demonstrate that I have up-to-date knowledge of the field as it is today.

Because the administrative field is evolving at a breakneck speed, professional certifications that offer real-world, up-to-date learning are highly valuable. Fortunately, there are a number of options for administrative certification. The two most popular are the Certified Administrative Professional (CAP) credential, provided by the International Association for Administrative Professionals (IAAP), and the Professional Administrative Certification of Excellence (PACE) credential, provided by the American Society for Administrative Professionals (ASAP).

NOTE: In the spirit of full transparency, I wrote two of the four modules for the PACE certification and I work closely with ASAP in delivering this program.

I often tell people the process of certification is as much about learning as it is about validating what you already know. Many organizations seek out professionals with these designations, and they provide added leverage for salary negotiation and advancement discussions.

It is important to note that there is a difference between a "certificate" program and a "professional certification."

Generally speaking, a *certificate program* is a learning opportunity in which participants receive a certificate after completing a course or series of courses; there is no requirement for ongoing learning to keep the certificate. In this way, it is similar to a degree in that it is a stagnant form of learning.

Alternatively, a *professional certification* typically requires a demonstration of mastery over the material, which usually involves some combination of proven field experience and an exam. Certifications are often overseen by an independent accrediting body that verifies the program meets credentialing standards.

Additionally, and perhaps most importantly, professional certifications *usually* have that ongoing learning requirement to maintain them. This is what makes them so attractive to employers.

Professional certifications and certificate programs are not the only option for learning. If you're not up for the time and financial investment they require, there are plenty of other professional development courses and training sessions you can engage in—many of which are quick and inexpensive (sometimes even free). Whether you prefer learning from the comfort of your desk or want to get out and learn with colleagues in your local community, you will find a wealth of options available, spanning a broad range of topics relevant to the field. Quality can vary dramatically, so always do your research to find the right courses that suit your needs.

Recently, conferences for administrative professionals have also grown in popularity. Ranging in size from less than a hundred participants to more than a thousand, these events typically last two to four days and include keynote presentations as well as small, breakout workshops. Conferences are a great opportunity to connect with like-minded career admins from around the world, while also enjoying a wide variety of field-specific training.

Admittedly, the financial aspect of learning is a concern for many. While free and low-cost options are great (and certainly better than nothing!), the more extensive, in-depth programs (such as large conferences) do require an investment, and sometimes a hefty one. As mentioned previously, more and more organizations are recognizing the value of devoting financial resources to their admin staff. But it is still a struggle for many. Leaders must be able to justify their expenses. If they are directing hundreds, or even thousands, of dollars toward administrative professionals, they must be able to clearly define the expected return on that investment.

If you're interested in participating in an educational endeavor, and you want your organization to fund it, your best bet is to create a comprehensive business case that describes exactly what you hope to achieve and how the learning will positively impact your team and organization.

Note: You can download a free Business Case Template on ElevateAdmins.com.

Remember, if at first you don't succeed, be *pleasantly* persistent. Budgets get reallocated, financial circumstances change, employee development initiatives come and go and then come back again. You never know what might be different this time around and how it might work in your favor.

Still, even a strong business case can't create money that isn't available. Should your request for funds be flatly declined, you still have other options. Sadly, many admins simply give up, which signals to leaders that the opportunity wasn't really worth it anyway.

If something is truly important, you should consider putting your own "skin in the game." Perhaps your company can pay a portion of the fees, and you can make up the difference from your own resources. A shared investment is a great way to make sure everyone has a stake in the outcome. Get creative if you need to. Maybe you can agree to pay all the fees in exchange for some additional paid days off in the future. You have a wide variety of options for making it work.

If all else fails, consider making the full investment yourself. As Earl Nightingale said, "Your company owns your job; you own your career." The things you learn are yours to take with you wherever you go. And investing in yourself always pays off. *You* are the most solid investment there is. The more you expand your skills and capabilities, the more you become a highly attractive asset for organizations. That means more opportunities and more earning potential.

To be clear, I recommend continued learning not because it will have some immediate, dramatic impact on your pay or promotion prospects. Yes, it can help—but it's not a guarantee. It's what you do with the learning, the added value you're able to deliver, that results in such rewards.

Instead of focusing on the tangible rewards of learning, I find it more useful to focus on the intangible benefits—the internal affirmation of your commitment to growth and development, and the external demonstration of this to others. In terms of building a career, these are more valuable than anything else.

Taking Ownership of Your Career

In 1997, a gentleman named Tom Peters wrote a (now famous) article for *Fast Company* magazine titled, "The Brand Called You." This was the first time the concept of *personal branding* was introduced to the world, and today this term has become part of our collective professional lexicon.

A key part of Peters' thesis is stated early in the article when he writes, "Regardless of age, regardless of position, regardless of the business we happen to be in....We are CEOs of our own companies: Me Inc."

At the time, this was a groundbreaking idea—to think of your career as a business and yourself as an owner. Perhaps this is something you've never considered. After all, most admins think of themselves as employees. While this is true in one sense, it is still far more valuable to take the mentality of an owner.

Think of it this way: In your business (your career), you provide services in exchange for payment. Right now, as an employee, you have one primary client (your organization). However, you are a marketable asset. At any point in time, you could choose to find a different primary client or offer a different array of services or do anything you'd like with your business.

To remain competitive and grow your business, you have to accept full responsibility over your career. After all, a business owner does not expect his or her clients to worry about the long-term success of the business. That's the owner's job. In your career, it's your job (not your boss's and not your organization's).

When it comes to your career, *you* are the ultimate authority. It is your right *and obligation* to prioritize your path. No one can do it for you. Do not abdicate your responsibility. There's too much at stake.

4

RAISING PERFORMANCE STANDARDS

I have a confession: I'm a recovering perfectionist.

I knew from an early age that my perfectionistic tendencies were problematic. I remember (while playing *Secretary*, in fact) writing and rewriting the same words over and over again in a notebook because I just couldn't manage to get my letters straight.

To this day, I truly struggle when writing by hand, as I constantly fight the temptation to do that.

Perfectionism can be debilitating. For many years, it stopped me from doing important things because I was convinced I couldn't meet my own unrealistically high performance expectations.

Over time, I came to understand my condition, and today, I consider myself "in recovery." I still have the persistent, almost obsessive desire for perfection in everything I do. But I've learned how to manage it. I continue to have extremely high expectations—for myself and others—but I no longer allow them to verge into unrealistic territory.

I share all of this as a preface to the following discussion because I know the performance standards for which I advocate are very high. However, I do not want that to intimidate anyone. For my fellow perfectionists, please understand the framework described in this chapter is aspirational. I do not know if it can ever truly be "mastered." View it is a tool for focusing your energy. Everyone will find they naturally excel in some areas and need improvement in others. As soon as you think you've conquered one element, you will discover it possesses a previously unknown layer of depth that requires further exploration.

Just as the field is constantly evolving, so are you. I encourage admins to never get complacent when it comes to performance. We should strive to continuously raise the bar, and at the same time, keep our expectations reasonable.

My hope is that this framework will inspire you and help you better understand the capabilities and related knowledge you need to perform at the highest levels as an administrative professional—to become an "elevated" admin. Let this serve as a guide for your continued growth and a barometer by which to measure your own competence.

The ELEVATE Admins Competency Model™

When I began training administrative professionals in 2009, I went on a search for a well-established framework defining the specific competencies required for peak performance in the field. Being the perfectionist I am, I was unable to identify one that I felt truly encompassed the full breadth and depth of the role. So, I decided to create my own.

Figure 2. The ELEVATE Admins Competency Model

The original version of this was first developed in 2010, but it has seen many revisions since—the most recent in August of 2020. I can only presume it will undergo more changes in the future as the field continues to evolve.

This is a product of my experience, observations, and research. Over the years, my coaching clients and training participants have weighed in and added their perspectives to help shape my thinking. I have received feedback on it from admins at all levels, as well as executives, HR leaders, and talent development professionals.

The model combines a number of elements, including personal attributes, knowledge, and behavior. (Those last two are what I broadly refer to as "competencies.") Though it may look overwhelming at first glance, when dissected piece by piece, it becomes much more manageable. So, let's break it down.

Note: For your convenience, you can find an at-a-glance reference table that outlines the key elements of each part of the Competency Model on ElevateAdmins.com.

Qualities

The bottom layer represents the foundation—the individual traits that make someone a successful administrative professional. These qualities are divided into three categories: character, ethics and professionalism.

CHARACTER describes who you are as a person—your work ethic, your values, and the overall level of care and interest you bring to your work. The most successful admins believe deeply in supporting and serving their team to the best of their ability; they are naturally compelled to help others, sometimes even to their own detriment. (We'll talk more about this later.) They possess an intense desire to perform well in the workplace and take true pleasure in professional success. The fact that you're reading this book is a strong indication you already have the kind of character I'm describing.

ETHICS has to do with integrity and your moral compass. As an administrative professional, you are entrusted with a lot of confidential and sensitive information related to your organization, its employees, and the business being conducted. One of the most critical functions of the role is the ability to protect privacy and diplomatically navigate complex situations while maintaining a strong ethical foundation. Your ability to do this is not only vitally important for maintaining trust with the person or people you support; it also helps set a powerful example for the rest of the team.

PROFESSIONALISM refers to your demeanor and self-presentation. This includes attitude, poise, language, physical appearance, and overall workplace behaviors. A true professional understands that everything you do (or don't do) influences how people see you and thus, the level of respect they afford you. Top administrative professionals display a calm, confident image, even when under tremendous pressure. They are able to think fast and stay optimistic, no matter the difficulties that arise. When team members are under stress, they are compassionate and reassuring, while at the same time, not overly emotionally invested. They possess a thick skin and do not let others jeopardize their composure.

To be clear, I am not suggesting successful administrative professionals are a homologous group or that you must adopt a certain personality type or workstyle. Authenticity and diversity are, indeed, important elements as well. However, certain behaviors are expected for those who want to perform at peak levels. There is no way around it.

I argue that *anyone* can develop these traits through practice, though they may come easier to some than others. Certain people are more naturally equipped to be successful in this role. Those who do not inherently possess these qualities may find them difficult to obtain—but they are essential. This is the foundation upon which your entire admin career is built. Cutting corners here endangers everything that follows.

Core Competencies

The next level up represents the core competencies, which are the building blocks for administrative work. The skill groups listed here are probably not surprising for those who have any level of experience in the field. They are all commonly cited performance requirements.

However, the goal is not simply to obtain proficiency in these areas, but rather, to acquire *advanced* proficiency. As John D. Rockefeller once said, "The secret to success is to do the common things uncommonly well." While the core competencies may appear straightforward on the surface, they are actually quite nuanced, as seasoned admins will surely attest.

The core competencies are:

ORGANIZATION: *The ability to maintain control over your physical environment.*

For administrative professionals, organization is about both perception and productivity. It is a functional necessity; without it, you can't be efficient or effective in your role. But beyond that, your organizational skills are a reflection of who you are as a professional. Whether right or wrong, others judge us by what's visible. Your organizational habits (or lack thereof) can speak volumes about your competence, ambitions, maturity, focus and more. Plus, as an administrative professional, you are also a reflection of the person or people you support, so these judgments can easily spread to them as well.

Admins have three areas in which they must develop and leverage effective organizational routines:

1. **Paper**. While the promise of a paperless workplace is enticing, the reality is that some amount of paper will probably always be necessary. Managing paper in the office is like managing laundry at home: it's a never-ending chore. If you don't stay on top of it, things pile up and cause major confusion. Mishandled and misplaced paperwork, especially that which contains confidential information, can be potentially very damaging and costly to the business. Part of your job is to create and leverage effective organizational systems for accurately storing and retrieving paperwork so it's easily and quickly accessible to the right people at the right times.

2. **Physical Space**. Your workspace has a significant impact on your performance. Research from the Princeton University Neuroscience Institute suggests that the more cluttered and chaotic your environment is, the more distracted and unfocused you are likely to become. Throughout the course of any given day, your work area will likely accumulate a lot of *stuff*. That's to be expected. The goal is not to maintain a perfectly empty space. Rather, it is keep the space orderly and return it to a tidy

condition at the end of each day. The same goes for all work areas over which you are responsible.

I argue these same principles apply for home offices. Even though few people may actually see your space, you will still feel the impact of it. And arguably, at home, work notes and other paperwork are even more likely to "go missing" if your space is not carefully managed.

3. Virtual Space. As paper becomes less prevalent in the modern workplace, there will be a greater emphasis on maintaining an organized virtual space, which includes managing digital files and minimizing electronic clutter. As an admin, your virtual space is highly visible; in the office, anyone can look over your shoulder and view what's happening on your screen. During an online meeting, you could be asked to share your screen, and suddenly your virtual world is on display for all to see!

I have known admins with computer desktops that were literally *covered* with files overlapping one another. I couldn't imagine how they found anything—but all of them claimed to have a "system." Sadly, that's not enough. People judge your virtual environment, just as they do your physical environment. You need to follow established best practices (including organizational policies) for naming, storing, organizing, and purging digital files—otherwise, the sheer volume will eventually overwhelm you.

TIME AND PROJECT MANAGEMENT: *The ability to appropriate allocate the right time to the right activities.*

There's always too much to do and not enough time; this is a chronic complaint of nearly every professional. Everyone is looking for ways to get more done in less time. From tracking deadlines and setting priorities to overseeing complicated projects with dozens of moving parts, you must learn how to fit ever-increasing demands into ever-shrinking pockets of time.

As an admin, your job is doubly hard. You're expected to manage time not only for yourself but for the person or people you support as well. This includes learning the delicate art of managing up and the vital techniques involved with managing expectations. For some, it also includes high-trust activities like managing the calendar and triaging email.

Time management is a complex and multifaceted field of study; it's an ideal example of the point I made earlier about releasing any lingering notions of perfection as you explore this model. This is one area where mastery may, indeed, be an unattainable myth.

I have yet to meet anyone—not a single soul at any level—who feels their time management skills are second to none. Nearly everyone has times in which they feel especially capable, focused, and productive. But these periods are usually short-lived, and often quickly followed by equally intense bouts of overwhelm, procrastination, and distraction.

Time management is not about *never* getting off track. I prefer to emphasize the importance of self-awareness. For admins especially, it's about *recognizing* when things are off track (or better yet, when they're headed that way) and quickly adjusting course to get back where you want to be. The workplace is far too unpredictable to ever expect anything more of ourselves or others.

It's also not about obsessing over the hot "tips and tricks" of the day. Rather, it's about understanding the underlying principles of effective time management. When you really know how to leverage systems, develop processes, streamline workflow, and properly prioritize competing demands, you're able to address time issues at their core, rather than cover them up with a temporary quick fix.

I consider project management (PM) an element of the time management competency, though it is, in itself, an entire field of study and a profession of its own. However, administrative professionals often operate as "unofficial" project managers, overseeing (at times) incredibly complex, high-impact, cross-functional projects. They often do so without any formal PM training or direct authority over project team members, making it all the more challenging.

I believe wholeheartedly that PM is one of the most valuable areas of study for administrative professionals. While *tasks* may be easily automated in the future, *projects* (which involve an interconnected series of tasks) will continue to require human oversight. Gaining expertise in this area is a key way in which admins can differentiate themselves and provide added value in the role.

COMMUNICATION: *The ability to interact appropriately with others.*

Communication is truly the make or break skill of the core competencies. It is the one skill that will enhance all others, and when it is lacking, no other skill can make up for it. Regardless of your proficiency in other areas, if you're unable to effectively communicate, you will not achieve peak levels of performance in this career.

As an administrative professional, you interact with people at all levels inside and outside the organization. Without strong communication skills, you run the risk of creating all kinds of difficulties for yourself and others, including but not limited to:

- Misunderstanding needs and failing to deliver what is expected
- Experiencing conflict with coworkers, clients, and/or superiors
- Struggling to get people to listen and respond to your requests
- Wasting time, energy, and resources on unnecessary back and forth

Ultimately, your communication capabilities have the power to positively or negatively impact your professional reputation and your ability to get things done.

Understanding communication styles is a critical component for success in this area. Knowing your own natural style is a good first step, but equally important is the ability to identify the styles of others. Beyond that, you need to use this information to adapt your behaviors when interacting with people and, in essence, learn to communicate in "their language."

As an admin, adaptation is an essential aspect of the role. You are a support professional, and your job is to help others succeed. Consequently, you may need to sacrifice your own communication preferences to ease your interactions with the person or people you support. Doing so is both respectful and effective, and it's a sign of emotional maturity on your part. Once you are able to confidently do this, you will discover you can create strong working relationships with literally *anyone*. There is truly no feeling more empowering.

Communication is a very broad knowledge area. It's about more than just words; it also involves paying attention to body language and tone of voice (your own and that of others) to help transmit your intended message and properly interpret the messages of others. At the same time, you must learn to be clear and concise across all modes of communication—phone, email, etc.

Administrative professionals must take an active role in developing strong communication routines with the person or people they support, which often involves establishing regularly scheduled meetings. It is the admin's responsibility to demonstrate the value of this time by arriving prepared, asking questions, and actively listening. Above all, admins must get comfortable initiating communication, rather than waiting for it to be offered. This is a key performance differentiator, and an important skill business leaders not only *want* from their support staff, but *need*.

CLIENT SERVICE: *The ability to deliver value to those you serve.*

Client service may be the most unexpected component of the core competencies. Often, administrative professionals see this and immediately resist the idea. "My job is not client service!" they say. But I beg to differ.

Clients can be internal or external. As an admin, you provide service to people within your organization, on your team and others, as well as people outside of the organization. But your primary client is the person (or people) you support. This can be a major mindset shift for some admins, but once you see it this way, you'll realize that client service is, indeed, the essence of your role.

If you want to be a little more technical, you can say that the admin role is to both serve *and protect* the person or people you support. I know this is law enforcement terminology, and I'm not suggesting you should be literally jumping in front of bullets for them. But figuratively, that's what you do all day! Admins protect time and attention. They act as gatekeepers and ensure organizational leaders are not distracted by the copious number of people and situations vying for their attention on a minute-by-minute basis.

Gatekeeping is a particularly difficult skill because, even as you're directing people *away* from your leaders, you still must ensure that everyone feels cared for and their needs are met. This requires exceptional communication skills (as previously discussed), the ability to listen with empathy and compassion, and an unwavering solution-focused attitude.

Ultimately, emotional intelligence is the key to successful client service. Learning how to recognize your own emotions, as well as the emotions of others, and how to appropriately manage your response to them, is what makes it possible for you to effectively handle the complex, and sometimes intense, situations for which your clients turn to you for support.

TECHNOLOGY: *The ability to utilize expertise with necessary work equipment.*

This fifth and final core competency is perhaps the most obvious, given our prior discussions regarding the evolution of the admin role and the rapidly changing technical landscape of today's business environment. To be clear, this is not about mastery of any one specific tech tool; it's about attaining broad technological acumen.

There is a parable, known as, "The Swordless Warrior," which I think offers an apt analogy. I first discovered this in the book, *The 5 Choices: The Path to Extraordinary Productivity*, by Kory Kogon, Adam Merrill, and Leena Rinne. Here is a paraphrased version of the story:

 A tired and worn-out soldier who has lost his sword stumbles across the battlefield, looking for a weapon he can use. He sees the top of another sword sticking out of the ground and quickly rushes to pick it up. Pulling it out of the ground, he finds the sword is broken and throws it to the side in disappointment.

"If only I had the Emperor's shining, gold sword!" he cries, "Then I could win this battle!"

A moment later, another tired soldier arrives and sees the same broken sword. He quickly grabs it and thrusts it excitedly into the air. With renewed vigor, he shouts to his men and returns to battle, using the broken sword to lead his army to victory.

The moral of this story is simple: We must not get attached to having the "perfect" tools. It is far better to be able to use *any* tool at our disposal to win the battles we face.

This lesson is especially relevant in the tech arena. The tools available are always changing and seldom are they perfect. Rather than focus our energy on one specific tool, we should instead learn how to use whatever tools we have to the best of our ability. This is what it means to be "tech savvy."

I consider the following ten traits indicative of a tech savvy professional:

1. Strives to keep his or her skills up-to-date at all times
2. Adopts new technology quickly
3. Experiments with emerging technology using trial and error
4. Leverages self-help tools and training resources to troubleshoot
5. Looks for new ways to leverage technology to improve efficiency
6. Effectively filters information so as to prevent overload

7. Understands the fundamentals of internet research and determining reliable sources
8. Follows appropriate digital etiquette when interacting electronically
9. Effectively uses tech tools to build and maintain relationships remotely
10. Adheres to best practices for cybersecurity

This list may look overwhelming, but the demands are high for modern admins. In many ways, the experience of 2020 forced each of us to embody these ten traits without even realizing it!

The primary point is that you shouldn't fear technology; instead, approach it with both a playful sense of curiosity and a recognition of its shortcomings. Technology has the potential to help us or hinder us; how we choose to interact with it will determine our outcomes.

Advanced Competencies

Looking again at the Competency Model, the next level up includes six "slices" in a pie-shape. These are the advanced competencies, which (as the name suggests) are the skills and knowledge required for higher-level administrative work. These are the skills that truly separate an average support professional from an administrative *partner*. They are especially important for those seeking advanced roles, such as C-Suite executive assistant, chief of staff, office manager, and so on.

That being said, it's never too early to focus on the advanced competencies. Even those who are new to the field will benefit from exploring these topic areas. Additionally, it may take some time to truly gain proficiency, so the sooner you can start, the better.

Just above the pie slices, you'll notice the words "Critical + Creative Thinking." This indicates that each of the six advanced competencies require two levels of mental processing.

Critical thinking refers to the use of logic and reasoning. Creative thinking refers to that which is more abstract and, to use a popular buzz-term, "outside the box." Both cognitive skillsets require the ability to investigate, reflect, and make connections that aren't always obvious.

All of the advanced competencies require focused attention and a conscious effort to avoid succumbing to "autopilot." This is what happens when you go through the physical motions of an activity, without really engaging in it mentally. For example, you drive yourself to work, pull into your parking space and suddenly think, "Who drove here?"

This kind of routine, subconscious activity is perfectly fine (and even useful) in some areas of life and work. It saves precious mental energy, which is not required in every, tiny task of the day. But to elevate your role as an admin, you must not allow yourself to spend *too much* time here. When operating on autopilot, you're more likely to miss important details. You're performing based on habit, not based on the true needs of the situation. And this can get you into trouble! These advanced competencies require your full mental engagement.

BIG PICTURE UNDERSTANDING: *The ability to interpret the broad business environment.*

This skill is all about context. It involves observing what's happening around you and recognizing how things interconnect. When you understand the big picture, you're able to appreciate how actions create consequences, and how any one choice can cause ripple effects that spread far and wide throughout the organization. In recent years, these concepts have been broadly labelled, "systems thinking."

Administrative professionals tend to struggle with this skill; I would venture to say it's the most difficult aspect of the Competency Model for many. After all, admins are revered for their attention to detail. It's common practice to put on your figurative "blinders" and focus solely on your slice of the world. When you try to widen your perspective, it can feel overwhelming. Additionally, many admins (particularly those at lower levels) do not have easy access to information. Even if they *want* to understand the big picture, they are often left in the dark.

However, without big picture understanding, you cannot perform at advanced levels—in fact, even basic performance can be jeopardized. Consider the daily necessity of prioritizing. Every admin must learn how to take an overflowing list of competing demands and identify which should be done now versus which can be strategically postponed.

Big picture understanding helps you make the right choices (i.e., the ones that create the most positive and/or least negative consequences for all involved). To prioritize effectively, you must understand what else is going on—other deadlines, dependent tasks, schedules of people involved, etc.—as well as the broad implications of what you're doing and not doing.

It's no exaggeration to say that big picture understanding is an *absolute requirement* for every other advanced competency. Without it, you cannot *effectively* improve processes, solve problems, make decisions, anticipate needs, or champion change. You can try, but you're likely to create problems for yourself (and possibly others) if you're not also considering the big picture.

Admittedly, getting the information you need can be difficult. This is where you must lean in to those communication skills discussed earlier. Ask direct questions—actively seek out information from a multitude of sources. You're not being nosy; you're simply attempting to acquire the knowledge you need to make intelligent choices on behalf of the person or people you support. Being a detective is part of your job. You can also leverage your fellow administrative professionals. Each of you will likely have a different piece of the big picture. Just like a puzzle, when you put the pieces together, you will all get a more accurate and complete view.

Finally, realize you cannot and will not ever know *everything* going on at your organization—and that's perfectly okay! The goal is not to create some static understanding of the big picture. Rather, the goal is to continually expand your understanding as the big picture continually shifts around you.

PROCESS IMPROVEMENT: *The ability to identify and implement ways to achieve greater impact.*

In many workplaces, people do things the way they've always done them *because that's the way they've always done them.* Someone taught them a process years ago, when they first started in the role perhaps, and they've done it that way ever since.

Rarely do we take the time to reevaluate our established ways of doing things (unless there's a problem!), but when we proactively stop and question our methods, we often find ample opportunity for improvements.

This skill is all about looking for those opportunities. Administrative professionals are in a prime position to identify ineffective and inefficient processes. More importantly, they are also the best people to find and implement improvements.

Whether it's a process that's unnecessarily complicated or one that's not creating the right results, don't be afraid to question the status quo. Things don't necessarily have to be broken before you fix them. Even if something is technically working, you can still ask, "How can we make this work *better*? How can we improve our outcomes? How can we make this easier, or faster, or more profitable?"

As technology continues to evolve, you may find more and more process elements can be automated or simply eliminated altogether. Don't worry! You're not streamlining yourself out of a job. You're adding value to the organization and freeing yourself to do more in other areas. And if you don't do it, someone else eventually will.

The overall theme of this competency can best be described as "kaizen." This Japanese word translates to "continuous improvement" and is a well-known philosophy adopted in many business environments. Toyota, for example, is frequently cited as an organization which leverages kaizen. Line personnel are instructed to stop production if and when they encounter abnormalities, and (in collaboration with leaders) they are expected to make suggestions for how to resolve them.

Kaizen supporters believe continuous improvement must come from all levels of the organization. The people working with the processes are the ones who will best know how to make positive changes to them.

Even if no one else in your organization has ever heard of kaizen, you can still be an advocate for this way of thinking and behaving. In doing so, you can help elevate your entire team.

PROBLEM-SOLVING: *The ability to find solutions for difficult or complex issues.*

This is yet another skill for which admins are perfectly positioned. In your role, you are inundated with problems all day long, from the simple to the mind-bendingly complex.

Your leader needs to be in two places at once? That's a problem.

You have twenty executives arriving for a meeting but the conference room is double-booked? That's a problem.

The presentation materials you painstakingly put together for the past week require a major correction, and you now have an hour to get them redone? That's a problem.

It happens all day, every day.

While your primary goal is to prevent problems proactively, some problems are unpredictable and unpreventable.

Therefore, you also have to be flexible enough to make things work even when they're not ideal. In many ways, the admin role, especially at higher levels, is an endless stream of problem-solving. You're constantly doing, undoing, and redoing. You're making plans, revising them, and revising some more. Things are constantly shifting, and your job is to fix the gaps that appear as that shift takes place.

As important as this kind of day-to-day problem solving is, there's a deeper level required as well. Problems that are part of a recurring pattern, for example, should be explored with a more critical eye. Instead of simply solving *the situation*, you also have to figure out *why* it's continuing to happen. Is there a deeper root cause that must be addressed? Sometimes, it may go back to an ineffective process. Other times, it may lead back to a person, a miscommunication or a problematic behavior. Proficiency in the problem-solving skillset means you're able to identify the source of the problem and offer a solution that not only fixes it, but doesn't cause *additional* problems along the way.

Notice that last point: offer *"a* solution," not *"the* solution." This is critically important. You don't have to come up with the end-all-be-all solution. If you can't fix a problem on your own, your goal is to present possibilities.

I discovered this early on in my admin career. Back then, when I found problems, I would often take them to my executive and ask him what to do. Inevitably, he'd say, "What do you suggest?"

I remember thinking at the time, "You're the boss! Aren't you paid the big bucks to figure these things out?"

But I quickly learned my lesson. He was training me to think things through and come up something—*anything*—to help him get going. If there's one thing I know, it's this: executives abhor a blank slate. Give them some options to start with, even if they aren't perfect. Ideally, you want to be able to say something like this: "Here's the problem and here are three ways we can solve it. I like option B best because of X, Y, Z reasons. What do you think?"

If all else fails and you simply can't come up with an adequate solution, you can always share the options you considered, and why you don't think they will work. Again, it's better than nothing.

Problem-solving is, in my opinion, one of the things that makes the admin career so exciting. It keeps things interesting! It forces you to use your brain and challenges you to think in new and different ways. I strongly believe that, if you're not encountering problems, you're not paying attention. They're all around you, and that's one of the reasons you are so vital.

DECISION-MAKING: *The ability to come to a conclusion using sound judgement.*

Here we have a skill that admins new to the field may find surprising. After all, "lack of decision-making authority" is a common complaint among less experienced support professionals. While I contend that even lower level admins have more decision-making opportunities than they often take advantage of, those in advanced roles will certainly understand both the power and importance of this skill.

As you rise through the higher levels of admin, decision-making capabilities become more essential with each step. Not only are you making decisions in the course of carrying out your daily responsibilities, but you're also frequently making decisions *on behalf of* the person or people you support. Some of these may appear fairly insignificant on the surface, though (at times) they can have unexpectedly dramatic ramifications. Others may have immediate, clear, and far-reaching consequences. It is therefore critical that you demonstrate sound judgement in all decisions, regardless of size or scope.

Ultimately, your decision-making should be motivated by integrity and a sincere desire to create the best possible outcomes. You want to make decisions you can reasonably defend. If someone questions your choices, you can provide a solid rationale. You always want to have a clear understanding of the expected results and the consequences of your decisions.

One of the best ways to build your skills in this area is to learn how your leaders make decisions. Discuss their thought process with them; be a sounding board. Find out what's most important to them and how they evaluate options. As time goes on, you will slowly gain a deeper understanding for how they think, and develop a similar decision-making style. Your own confidence will grow, just as their confidence *in* you will grow, and this will create more opportunities for you to flex and stretch your decision-making skills.

Thankfully, the more practice you get in this area, the more naturally the right decisions will come. You build an instinct for it. You can start to rely more on your own experience and even gut feelings. Still, it's important to remember that intuition only goes so far. Listen to it (don't ignore it), but don't trust it entirely. You always want a logical explanation for your decisions. In the business world, "It just felt right," isn't a valid justification.

ANTICIPATION OF NEEDS: *The ability to be proactive.*

When I ask executives to describe the qualities they want in their administrative partners, "anticipation of needs" is always at the top of the list. Of course, they don't normally use those words. More often than not, they say something like this: "I want my admin(s) to stay two steps ahead of me." Some jokingly ask if "mind-reading capabilities" are too much to hope for.

This is the essence of being proactive. Put another way, you can think of it like this: Being proactive involves doing the right things today to set yourself (and your leaders) up for success tomorrow. It's all about looking ahead, preparing for what's next, and taking initiative to do whatever needs to be done —*without necessarily being told.*

This is the skill that makes it possible for some admins to appear as if they can, indeed, read their partners' minds. They don't need direct communication about every little thing; they are so in sync, the admin is able to predict what's needed and handle it, often before the executive even has time to think of it.

For many admins, this skill requires a dramatic paradigm shift. To successfully anticipate needs, you must think beyond the immediate task at hand, and instead, focus on the end-result you're trying to achieve.

For example, if your executive asks you to schedule a meeting, that's the task, but it's not the ultimate goal. Helping your executive have a successful, productive meeting is the result you're truly after. To make that happen, you need to think through steps beyond just scheduling the meeting.

Based on your past experience, you can probably guess that a number of additional things need to happen to make this meeting successful and productive—a conference room must be booked, materials must be prepared, your executive may need time to review those materials, and so on. These are all needs you can anticipate; there's no reason to wait for specific instruction.

You might not automatically know everything that's needed or the specific details for each individual thing, but you can often figure it out based on predictable patterns of the past. If a meeting like this has taken place before, that becomes your roadmap. Or, at the very least, you can proactively request the information you need, rather than waiting for it to be offered.

Anticipating needs is like trying to decipher the picture on a puzzle when you don't have all the pieces. You have to be able to fill in the gaps on your own. It's a complicated skill that takes intentional practice to develop. But it's also one that will be noticed and very appreciated once you've mastered it.

If this is not already an area of strength for you, please consider grabbing my book, *The Proactive Professional* (available on Amazon) for a more detailed discussion of this topic and practical strategies for enhancing your skills.

CHANGE CHAMPIONSHIP: *The ability to advocate for (and support others in adopting) necessary change.*

The final advanced competency is a reflection of the modern business environment and the critical role admins play in the organizational change process.

We all understand change is inevitable; if 2020 taught us nothing else, we at least gained an appreciation for the certainty of uncertainty.

But more than that, change is *necessary* for any organization to survive long term. It's no exaggeration to say that admins have the power to make or break change initiatives.

I've seen it happen many times over again: When the administrative team is not on board with something, they can bring everyone else down as well. Alternatively, when the admin team *is* on board, they can rally the rest of the team around it as well.

Administrative professionals often don't understand the power they wield. Yet, as any superhero fan knows, with great power comes great responsibility.

Change is naturally difficult for most people. We are biologically hardwired to resist it. After all, for our cavemen ancestors, environmental changes meant almost certain death. Our bodies evolved to react to change with a physiological stress response —commonly known as Fight, Flight, or Freeze. In today's business world, the changes we experience are not likely to be life threatening, but we still have the same instinctive response.

Embracing the skill of change championship means a number of different things. To begin, you must be able to manage your own natural response to change so you can adapt quickly and productively to it. As previously mentioned, others look to you as a bellwether. If you take change in stride, they are more likely to follow suit. If you panic, they will panic.

This can be especially hard because, in your role, you don't always have control over the changes that are made. You may suddenly arrive to work one morning and discover a company reorg is underway. You may be given a new set of procedures to follow or a new software to use without any explanation as to why. You may find yourself impacted by any number of changes that don't make sense or with which you don't necessarily agree. Regardless, you always have a responsibility to demonstrate an optimistic, make-it-work attitude. You don't know what you don't know, and you must have faith that your leaders have made decisions based on the best interests of the organization.

Beyond that, change championship also involves supporting others as they go through change, helping them to manage their resistance and come to terms with what is happening. This may mean communicating information to reduce confusion, helping them overcome obstacles as they implement changes, or simply being a supportive listener as they vent about the stress they are feeling. It is important to remember that everyone will move through the emotions associated with change at their own pace. You can provide encouragement and support, but you can't do it for them. Eventually, most people will grow to accept whatever changes come their way, and those who don't will move on.

Another element of change championship is supporting leaders as they roll out changes. All too often, organizational changes are handled poorly. Communication is lacking and information is sparse; consequently, employees feel blindsided and their feelings of resistance and uncertainty amplify immensely.

As an administrative professional, you are in an ideal position to help avoid this common occurrence. Because of your unique vantage point, you understand the concerns of the team and also have access to leadership. By getting involved in the change management process, you can be a powerful conduit for information. For example, if a change is not being well received, you can help leaders understand why. Perhaps the messaging is wrong, or maybe the change itself was ill-conceived, and the leaders need a different perspective to understand that. Whatever the case, your involvement can have a positive impact on change initiatives throughout the organization.

Lastly, change championship also includes having a voice in change initiatives, and being able to identify and advocate for necessary change. While there are many types of organizational change, admins are most ideally positioned to identify those related to systems, processes, people, and culture. Of course, not all changes require advocacy; some may be well within the scope of your ability and authority to simply make them. However, other changes may require approval or acceptance (and possibly even funding)—and this is where advocacy comes in.

In some cases, advocating for change may be as simple as making a suggestion to the appropriate decision-maker. In other cases, however, you may need to present a well-crafted, persuasive argument backed by data and evidence to convince the necessary parties that your change is worth exploring. While you might not gain immediate agreement, the exercise itself can spark important conversation, and it can also be a useful visibility booster for you.

While this may feel outside the realm of traditional "admin" work, it is a highly valuable added benefit that advanced administrative partners provide to their leaders. I have worked with many admins who have initiated incredible changes that have yielded quantifiable returns for their organizations; we will explore some of these stories in chapter 7. I believe that, as the admin field continues to evolve, such activities will become more commonly expected. For now, they are still seen as exceptional. Take advantage of that! Do the exceptional work and create an exceptional career.

Key Integrated Behaviors

The last element of the Competency Model can be found in the grey band around the outer-edge of the graphic. These are key behaviors that must be integrated into every other piece of the model. They are broad skillsets that truly define the final essential factors for peak performance in this role.

Teamwork

Unfortunately, many administrative professionals do not consider themselves part of a team. Those at lower levels tend to see themselves as *supporting* a team—they exist on the outside. Those at higher levels frequently feel separated due to their partnership(s). They support leaders, but aren't necessarily viewed as part of the leadership team. Additionally, admins are often scattered throughout organizations, supporting different departments and executives, and they may rarely gather together as a group. All of these factors can create a sense of isolation. As remote work and hybrid roles become more common, this feeling is likely to grow.

Moreover, admins who do operate within a collective work unit (or even just in close physical proximity to one another) often experience a high level of dysfunction. Territorialism, cliques, and interpersonal conflict are common complaints. These issues not only harm performance and productivity, they also damage the overall reputation of admins within the organization and as a professional group.

As difficult as it may be to accept, your success relies on more than just *you*. No man (or woman) is an island, especially in the workplace. As an administrative professional, you have the opportunity to play on multiple teams. Do not position yourself as an outsider; you hold a critical role among the people you support. Be an active participant. Work from a place of inclusion, and others will follow your lead.

Additionally, you and your fellow admins—no matter where they are in the organization—have the ability to form a powerful team. In combining forces, each individual wins. As the old saying goes, "A rising tide lifts all boats." A cohesive admin team can achieve remarkable results when the petty, unnecessary, and unprofessional drama is left behind.

Your job is to model elevated team behavior. Work to create a sense of equity among the group. Encourage people to lean on one another for support, leverage the wisdom of their teammates, and offer abundant peer recognition. Demonstrate the fundamental principles of respect, acceptance, and trust, and practice your advanced communication skills to resolve conflict constructively.

Sadly, there may be times when your efforts are not reciprocated by the group. Still, I encourage you to try. Even if the rest of the team just can't manage to get on board, you will have the comfort of knowing you did your part—and that will be evident to all who are watching.

One additional, though less obvious element of teamwork has to do with building your network inside and outside your organization. There are many instances in which you will need to leverage the support of people outside of your internal admin community to get things done. It is always beneficial to build relationships across your enterprise. Be a resource for people; help them achieve their goals. This kind of goodwill can come in handy in the future.

It's also smart to connect with people working at organizations yours does business with. For example, as an EA, I built relationships with the assistants of my boss's friends and business associates. When he needed something from them or wanted time on their calendar, I had an "inside" track to make it happen.

It's fair to say that relationships will make or break you in any field, but especially as an administrative professional.

Self-Management

While teamwork is an important part of the admin role, being able to work autonomously is equally important. Self-management is about taking responsibility for your own behaviors—guiding, motivating, and directing yourself, rather than relying on others to do it for you.

This is a hugely beneficial skill for administrative partners to master. Think of it this way: Your executives have limited resources of their own. They have a finite amount of time, energy, and attention to devote to an enormous number of activities. If they are spending a portion of their resources managing you, those resources can't be used elsewhere. When you embrace the idea of self-management, you allow your executives to free up their resources and redirect them to activities that deliver more value to the organization.

At the same time, self-management is a win for you. It allows you to have more control over your work and the ability to have a greater impact. With self-management, you experience true ownership over what you're doing, which provides a powerful sense of fulfillment.

To be clear, self-management is not the same as total self-reliance. You will still need the help of "management" at times.

But the goal is to reduce the amount of resources directed toward you as much as possible, work independently where you can, and demonstrate competence without supervision required.

Note: If you're struggling with a micromanager, this topic is covered in chapter 9.

LEADERSHIP

Once again, we have a quality that admins rarely associate with themselves. In fact, throughout the business world, leadership is frequently misunderstood. Most people think leaders are those who have a certain job title or hold a certain place in the organizational hierarchy. More broadly speaking, many believe leadership is all about ambitious ideas, big action, and impressive achievements. They think of leaders as larger-than-life celebrities, entrepreneurs, and political figures. And yes, there is an element of truth in all of this. But leadership is not necessarily any of these things. The concept itself is quite subjective.

As Kurt Uhlir, the CEO and cofounder of Sidequik once said, "Leadership comes from influence, and influence can come from anyone at any level and in any role."

Administrative professionals have an incredible opportunity for demonstrating influence within their teams and organizations. Every day, you help set the tone in the office. You lead others through your example, by being a resource and helping others to achieve their goals. You lead by gently guiding people where they need to go, by listening and questioning, and offering solutions.

Leadership is inherently a part of the admin role, and it is woven throughout the Competency Model.

For those who wish to advance in the admin field, this skill is particularly important. At higher levels, the person or people you support will rely heavily on you for your leadership. They will trust you, as their administrative partner, to tell them the difficult things they may not see on their own. They will give you authority to speak and act on their behalf. They will seek your counsel on issues and expect you to help them make wise decisions. All of this will come without glory and often without recognition from the world outside your office door.

It's not for the faint of heart. True leadership, at the advanced level, requires courage and self-sacrifice.

No matter where you currently are or what your aspirations may be, you have the power to be a leader in big ways and small. Don't underestimate the influence you have with your actions and your words. At the most basic level, leadership is about being a positive force for the people around you. And, at its most basic level, that's the job of an admin.

Putting It All Together

As you can see, the ELEVATE Admins Competency Model is a comprehensive framework that encompasses every major aspect of the role. While there may be minor variations within different organizations and industries, this covers the most common and most important elements across all levels *at the present time*.

I do my best to truly practice what I preach. As I encourage you, dear reader, to embrace a spirit of continuous improvement, I remind myself to do the same. This model, like everything I offer in this book, represents my current best thinking. My hope is to continuously expand my understanding of this field and what is required to be successful in it. Therefore, things are subject to change.

However, I can tell you with absolute certainty that, no matter what happens in the future, everything in this model will continue to serve you. Some elements may become more or less important, and new things may be added moving forward. But nothing will disappear. I believe the requirements for success in this role will only expand in the future; they will not shrink.

Remember that, in raising performance standards for yourself, you encourage those around you as well. Often, when one person on a team elevates, others realize their own need (or desire) to do the same. Please share this model with your colleagues.

Administrative professionals, as a group, are a tremendous source of untapped potential. When we broaden our thinking about what the role really is and what we have to contribute, we open a world of possibilities. When we expect more from ourselves and from our work, we find infinite capability—and that can never be adequately captured in any model.

5

DESIGNING A PARTNERSHIP

I n the process of becoming a certified career coach, I learned a concept called *intentional relationship design*. The idea is that, as a coach, the first thing you want to do with a client is sit down and discuss the kind of relationship you want to create together. You define your goals, establish boundaries, discuss communication methods, and so on. *Everything is on the table*. It's a powerful process that helps set the coach and the client up for success.

As an administrative professional, I had never heard of intentional relationship design. But I naturally employed a similar strategy. When I started my role as an executive assistant, I arrived with a whole list of questions for my new boss—about his priorities, his preferences, his personality, and much more. We spent two full days together just talking, getting to know one another, and figuring out what our relationship was going to be. I took an entire spiral-bound notebook full of notes!

I understand this kind of attention is a luxury few admins receive. It requires an investment of time and a commitment to the partnership. I was fortunate—but even with all of our early conversations, my executive and I still had plenty of struggles. Designing a strong partnership isn't just a one-time thing; it's an ongoing effort.

I believe the underlying principles of intentional relationship design are profoundly important, not just for coaches. If we want to create successful partnerships (with anyone), we must clearly define what success means and how we are going to work together to make it happen. Communication is the key.

As an administrative professional, relationships are at the center of everything you do, whether you're supporting a single executive or an entire team of people. You can't always sit down on your first day of work and gather all the information you need to craft the partnership you want. And even if you could, you'd inevitably have to redesign it over and over again. Nothing is stagnant, and partnerships are no exception. So, you have to learn how to weave the relationship design process into your regular work and make it a part of your normal routine.

What is a Partnership?

A partnership is a mutually beneficial relationship. By its very nature, it requires two or more parties—you can't have a partnership by yourself—and it's a two-way road. Everyone in the partnership needs to be invested, and everyone will reap the rewards.

A good partnership can be a competitive advantage for the executive and the organization as a whole. It allows both parties —the leader and the support professional—to do what they do best and contribute the kind of value for which they are each uniquely suited.

Here's where things get hard for administrative professionals: The kind of partnership you want may be different from the kind of partnership the person or people you support want. Both of you should have a say in the matter, but ultimately, it's their choice. After all, you're there to support them—so they define the kind of support they want.

I have personally worked for someone who did not want a true partner. He just wanted someone to take orders, do the admin work, and leave him alone as much as possible. I tried to show him what I could do, to educate him, and motivate him to try something different. But he didn't want it. Eventually, I had to move on, because I knew what I wanted, and I wasn't going to get it with him.

You can't build a partnership with an unwilling party. However, it's important to know that some people may *appear* unwilling when really, they just don't know what's possible, or they don't know how to go about building a partnership. That's where you come in!

Principles for a Powerful Partnership

Part of your role as an admin is to guide the partnership design/management process and make it easy for people to partner with you. Yes, your partners need to invest their time in this too, but you need to make sure it's time well used. Take responsibility and lead the way with these powerful partnership principles.

DEVELOP STRONG COMMUNICATION HABITS

One of the most common frustrations in the partnership between admins and executives is what I refer to as "mind reader syndrome." As the name suggests, this is where each person believes the other should just know exactly what they're thinking—no communication necessary.

In some ways, I worry that I perpetuate this condition. After all, I believe that, with the right skills, admins can learn to anticipate their leaders' needs—and this often creates the *illusion* of reading their minds. It is, indeed, just an illusion. And to ever get to this point, communication is absolutely necessary.

Executives must first be clear about what their needs and preferences are and, with time, admins can learn to anticipate predictable patterns. But not everything in the workplace is part of a pattern! New situations come up every day, and the executive's needs and preferences will slowly evolve. Even once you've supported the same person for years, you still won't be able to perfectly predict their every move.

Admins are equally afflicted with mind reader syndrome. They often believe their leaders should simply know what information they need, understand how long things take to do, or recognize when they're overloaded with too many urgent tasks. They don't want to actually talk about these things or make direct requests of their executives. They would much rather the execs simply know and accommodate accordingly.

As you read this, it probably sounds ridiculous. Of course, we all understand the impossible standard we set with this mind reader expectation. But I'm also betting that, as you read this, it feels all too familiar.

To break out of mind reader syndrome, you must become willing to communicate—probably much, *much* more than you are used to.

BE PROACTIVE

Though most professionals know communication is important, we often put in on the back-burner until there's a problem. We neglect it until suddenly we're *forced* to do it. At that point, we're not really connecting in a meaningful way; we're just trying to repair the damage and prevent things from getting worse. Once the storm has blown over, we usually go right back to our non-communicative ways.

This is a horribly reactive cycle, yet it's incredibly common among admins and the executives they support. It's understandable why this happens—everyone is busy! It's easy to fall into a pattern of speaking only briefly in passing. As an admin, you don't want to take time away from your leaders.

And leaders, unfortunately, just don't always think about communicating with their staff. Good old mind reader syndrome kicks in and we all expect we're on the same page, even when we're not.

However, to make a partnership work, there must be an open and ongoing dialogue between parties. Communication should not be reserved solely for times when things go wrong. In fact, if you communicate more frequently, there will eventually be fewer such times.

Proactive communication means you're communicating *before* there's ever a desperate need to do so. The best way to make this happen is by creating structures that encourage you to communicate on a routine basis. By doing this, there's never enough time for problems to fester. You're able to address potential issues early and prevent others from ever seeing the light of day.

Engage in Daily Stand-Up Meetings

Any administrative professional who has engaged in admin-specific professional development has likely heard this suggestion before. I repeat it here for the benefit of those who have not heard it, and also for those who need to hear it again. Sometimes, you have to receive the same message delivered in a few different ways to make it sink in.

Daily communication is an inescapable necessity for admins who support individual executives on a one-to-one basis. For those supporting groups of people, it is unrealistic to expect that you can meet with each individual every day, and it is also unnecessary. For you, daily communication should take place with one or two people, preferably those who are leaders within the group. They can help act as a funnel through which information flows between you and everyone else.

I recommend holding daily "stand-up" meetings. This name comes from the project management world and refers to the fact that these meetings are intended to be short; don't sit down and get comfortable. The purpose is to quickly review each person's goals for the day and make sure you're focused on the right things. During this time, each party can ask questions and make direct requests of the other. With this routine, you will ensure you're aligned on the day's priorities and prevent any roadblocks along the way.

Obviously, this kind of meeting is most beneficial first thing in the morning and face-to-face. However, every partnership is different. Some prefer to meet at the end of each day. Some have to meet over the phone or via video. Whatever works for you is fine. The important thing is that you are, in fact, meeting and communicating *every* day. Put it on the calendar and treat it as any other appointment.

I have worked with dozens of executive/assistant partner teams over the past ten years. When I suggest daily meetings, they inevitably scoff and claim it will be impossible given their busy schedules. I have yet to find a team for which that is true. There is *always* time if you're willing to make it.

I had one executive who ended up calling his assistant each morning on the drive into the office. That was the only way they could make it happen; once he set foot in the building, he was pulled in a million different directions. But over the phone, from the car, his assistant got his full attention. This simple change in their daily routine profoundly impacted their partnership. Almost immediately they felt more in sync and were able to get more done. After just a few months, each individual noted specific, measurable performance improvements. After a year, they both agreed their morning calls were essential, and they would never give them up.

Almost every partner team I've worked with has reported a similar positive response to this simple strategy. But oddly, many of them do not stick to the routine. Though they see the benefits of meeting daily, they fall back into bad habits, usually after only a few weeks.

Typically, it goes something like this: One person says, "I don't think we have anything to discuss today, so let's skip it." That happens for a few more days, and pretty soon, the entire structure has turned to dust.

Don't let that happen to you! Keep your routine. Meet every day —*even if you don't think you have anything to talk about.* More often than not, something will come up and the time will prove useful after all. Even if you truly have nothing to talk about, you still maintain your habit. You still demonstrate your commitment to one another and to the partnership. These times are perfect for discussing topics related to the "big picture" and proactively planning ahead.

Usually, it is the executive who will begin deprioritizing the daily meeting. The admin almost always wants it to happen. But if the executive doesn't see value, they have no reason to keep devoting energy to the process. Thus, it is imperative that the admin visibly show they are making good use of the time.

Always arrive organized and prepared, and give the meeting your full attention. Keep a running list of questions and discussion items. Have anything you need at your fingertips so you're not wasting time trying to find things. If you take it seriously, they will follow your lead.

Schedule Time for Deeper Discussions

Daily stand-ups are ideal for discussing specific, immediate work issues. But because they're intended to be quick, they don't work as well for more complex, abstract, or lengthy topics, or those which pertain to things taking place in the distant future. That's why, *in addition* to daily stand-up meetings, I also recommend scheduling time for deeper conversations.

In my first year as an assistant, my executive and I used to have weekly "State of the Union" meetings. These were scheduled times during which we discussed our partnership—what was working and what needed to change. We were still getting to know one another and this pre-booked time gave us a regular opportunity to just check in for a deeper chat, not focused on the specific work of the day, but focused on us.

As the partnership developed, we slowly started discussing other things as well. During our weekly chats, we would check in on long-term goals and discuss plans for the future, anywhere from a few weeks out to a few months and beyond. This allowed us to be more proactive, so we never felt like things were sneaking up on us. Sometimes, our discussions would wander off, and we'd end up talking about our families and our plans for the weekend. The agenda was fluid, but there was always plenty to fill the time—and it was always a valuable use of an hour.

For some partners, an hour a week may be too much to devote to this kind of meeting. It may make more sense to do it every other week or once a month. But you *do* need this time and it must be scheduled. Otherwise, it won't happen.

Remember that we're trying to create communication structures to get ahead of problems. It's easy to put this kind of thing off when everything is going smoothly. But don't wait until you have pressing issues that have to be addressed. By doing this now, you reduce the likelihood of those issues ever arising.

BUILD AND DEEPEN TRUST

Trust is an essential component of this partnership. Admins are deeply involved in their executives' work. Much of the time, they require access to highly confidential information and sometimes also *personal* information of the people they support. For the executive to release control and allow the admin to do the job, they must have a profound level of trust in that individual's competence and character.

At the same time, you, as the administrative professional, must also be able to trust your leaders. You are expected to go to great lengths to ensure they are successful. You are asked to make hard decisions and communicate difficult messages on their behalf. To assume the inherent risk involved, you must trust they are steering you well and will "have your back" should things go awry.

In short, both parties must know they're on the same team.

Trust is not something that magically appears overnight; it must be experienced over time.

New admins frequently struggle to accept this. They often want immediate trust from their executives, and are disappointed when certain projects or tasks are not handed over right away.

Without a proven track record, trust is not possible. Sure, they can have *faith* in your abilities, based on your history with others. But until they experience it themselves, it isn't trust.

I believe the most crucial factor in building trust is consistency. When you demonstrate the same behaviors over and over again, people know what to expect. If you've consistently been reliable in the past, it's reasonable to trust that you'll consistently be reliable in the future.

However, when you behave unpredictably, people have a much harder time trusting you. They don't know what to expect. Maybe you'll be reliable, or maybe you won't. Your past behavior has only proven it could go either way.

To help inspire trust, do your best to be consistent in your performance and your presence. Erratic, emotional impulsivity is not your friend! The more stable and steady you are, the more trustworthy you are.

But what if your executive is unpredictable? Does that mean you can't or shouldn't trust him or her? Admittedly, it's much harder to build trust in this situation. But I encourage you to remember there may be things happening beneath the surface that are impacting your executive's choices. Seek to understand why they are behaving the way they are. Is it circumstantial, or is it a reflection of character?

Shelby, a coaching client of mine, supported an executive who was constantly shifting direction. One day, he'd be all fired up about a new project, and the next day it would be cancelled. Over and over, Shelby would rearrange her priorities to try to keep up, only to find her efforts were all in vain. This happened so often, Shelby began to feel she couldn't trust her executive.

When she finally sat down to discuss it with him, she learned that the constantly changing direction had nothing to do with him. In fact, he was equally frustrated by it! The decisions were being made by someone above him. He was pushing back as much he could, but the situation was out of his control. After hearing Shelby's concerns, the executive agreed to be more transparent about things in the future. He couldn't alleviate the headaches, but he could understand her feelings. Together, they agreed to manage the situation as best they could.

Shelby's executive had a consistent character—he was a hard worker and a team player. He wanted to keep Shelby in the loop with new projects, but didn't want to bad-mouth a colleague when the plans changed so frequently. By opening up the discussion, Shelby was able to learn more, and her trust in her executive was renewed.

This brings me to another important point about trust: It is enhanced with communication and transparency. The more we can honestly share with one another, the more we will understand one another. Most people don't just act without cause. If we know the reasons behind the actions we're seeing, it all makes more sense. If we share what we are experiencing, we help others make more sense of us. Even if we don't always see eye to eye, we still gain appreciation for the other person's perspective.

Ironically, it takes trust to communicate with true transparency. At the same time, it builds trust. Don't be afraid to have the hard conversations, like my client Shelby did. Take a risk and you may be surprised by the payoff.

Remember You're Human

Executives and admins alike are both human. For some unknown reason, we all tend to forget that from time to time. We expect one another to behave like perfectly predictable robots.

Humans are interesting creatures—each inherently valuable and inevitably flawed. We all have our weird personality quirks and little pet peeves. We all have deeply multifaceted lives, which include many other things outside of work, and we all have bad days. We all have concerns about family, health, and money. We all go through periods of unrelenting stress and periods of unmitigated joy, and long stretches of something in between the two.

When you're working in partnership with someone, you cannot forget these things. Cut them some slack. Be quick to forgive and overlook the small stuff. Don't judge them too harshly for their imperfections; you have some too.

Remember that people are complicated and scarred. Sometimes, they allow bad experiences with others to taint how they look at you or how they treat you. But also remember that people can grow and change. Help them, and give them time.

The bond that forms between an executive and his or her administrative partner is unlike any other in the business world. With care and attention, it can become powerful beyond measure. It's no surprise that many executives and assistants will make career moves together, as a team. When the executive accepts a promotion, or moves to a new organization, it's a package deal. Whether or not that's the level you wish to attain, know that it is possible.

With the right partnership, there are no limits to what you can accomplish.

6

CAREER PATHS FOR ADMINS

I believe the admin role offers a wealth of opportunity for those who seek it. However, many administrative professionals tell me they don't know how to move forward in their career. They often attribute this to the fact that their company doesn't have a defined career path for the admin role.

This is really common in today's business world. The concept of linear career growth along a pre-defined path is becoming a thing of the past. Gone are the days when you'd join a company as a junior admin, and then two years later, you'd become an admin assistant, and then two years later you'd become a *senior* admin assistant, and two years after that you'd become an executive assistant and so on. That kind of straightforward, company-supported career progression still exists in some fields (like more traditional law firms and CPA firms), but it's not the norm in the admin world.

In most organizations, it is now considered the individual's responsibility to define his or her own career path. This goes for admins as well as many other roles. I think this is a wonderful thing because it empowers each of us to make our own career decisions.

However, it can also feel a little overwhelming, especially if you don't know what's possible and what career progression or advancement as an admin might look like. That's why I want to give you some structure to help you think about your career path and explore the opportunities for growth as an administrative professional.

Advancement vs. Progression

First, it's important to make a distinction between advancement and progression.

Career *advancement* traditionally involves a formal job or title change, while *progression* involves changes in duties. Much of the time, progression is a more informal process.

You could, theoretically, hold the same role at the same organization for many years. If, over that period of time, you took on a wide array of new responsibilities and accepted greater levels of authority, you could argue that your career progressed. Even though it is not reflected in your title, it could be reflected in your expanded job description, your accomplishments, the skills you've developed, and the experience you've gained.

Both advancement and progression are important for a number of reasons. The growth process, in and of itself, is very personally rewarding. As humans, we all crave challenge and find fulfillment in achieving new levels of success. Advancement is also a sign of success that is easily recognized by others—a new title can feel like an important status symbol. Plus, advancement often comes with a nice pay increase, which no one is going to complain about!

Additionally, being able to show forward movement in your career is useful for future employment. Prospective employers want to see visible career growth because it's a strong indicator that the person is not complacent. Depending on how much, what kind, and what rate of growth has taken place, it can also be a reflection of the person's character, ambition, and level of career commitment.

Over any considerable length of time (generally two or more years), recruiters and hiring managers want to see that you've grown in your career *in some way*.

Advancement is easy to see on a resume. You can quickly tell if someone's title or job has changed. Progression is a little harder to demonstrate on paper, but it certainly can be done.

It's worthwhile noting that growth doesn't always have to be in a single direction. While we often think of a career path as a ladder going straight up, in today's world it's more like a jungle gym. You can move to the side, or even backward at times, and still be "progressing" as long as your moves are purposeful. Whatever choices you make in your career, you always want to be able to explain your reasoning and how your choices helped you grow.

Opportunities for Growth

As I see it, growth for administrative professionals falls into two broad categories: you can grow your career in the admin field, or you can leverage your admin skills and grow your career in another field altogether.

ADMIN CAREER GROWTH

Many admins get their start supporting teams or groups of people. This is a good way to get your feet wet and see if admin is the right field for you.

The most common strategy for growth involves moving into supporting smaller groups in a deeper way, or individuals in a one-to-few or one-to-one partnership. Generally, this means taking on an executive assistant title.

From there, you can move on to supporting higher level individuals, perhaps moving from a director, to a VP, to a C-level executive. For many admins, supporting a CEO or someone else in the C-Suite can be a career pinnacle.

While this is the most traditional form of advancement in admin, you have other options as well. For example, you can concentrate on departmental expertise. So, instead of focusing on the person, you focus on the business function. Perhaps you specialize in supporting IT departments, or marketing, or finance. By focusing on the department or function, you develop expertise in a certain area of the business, so you can provide a deeper level of support. Admins with departmental expertise often get the opportunity to work on advanced projects that go far outside the scope of a traditional admin role.

Alternatively, you can focus your attention on honing a specific skillset. During my time as an office professional, I discovered my love of writing. In every role I held, I made special effort to develop this skill. In one job, I volunteered to write for the company website. In another, I actually created and edited a monthly client newsletter. I worked to became the go-to person for drafting all client communications. (In fact, I was rewarded with the title of Client Communications Manager, in addition to my title of Executive Assistant.) At the time, I had no idea that sharpening my writing skills would serve me so well in my future career endeavors! I just knew it was something I loved and wanted to do more of.

Admin offers a great diversity of work, so whatever skillset interests you, there are likely plenty of opportunities for practice.

Another option is to focus on administrative management. This role involves supervising and overseeing the work of other admins. People in this position may be called "chief of staff" or "director of administration," or they may hold a variety of other titles. This is a great path for people who are natural leaders or those who enjoy mentoring and developing others.

If you want to think on a grander scale, you can consider becoming a thought leader in the admin field. This involves sharing your expertise via articles, social media, or even live presentations at conferences. This is the path I (unknowingly) took while working as an executive assistant. Many people who still work full-time admin jobs also engage in field leadership in their off-hours. They consider it a rewarding bonus activity that offers personal and professional growth.

As an administrative manager or field leader, you need a variety of skills, many of which fall outside the typical admin skillset. In the next chapter, we'll discuss this more deeply and you'll read some interesting stories from people who have embraced administrative leadership in many different ways.

If you want to remain in the admin field, I hope you can now see it offers plenty of ways to grow. Whether you're looking to advance your career more traditionally or progress in a non-traditional fashion, you have a lot of options available to you.

EXPLORING OTHER FIELDS

Of course, admin might not be your field of choice for the long-term. That's perfectly okay too.

As mentioned previously, admin work is very diverse, which means your experience in this field provides you with a wide variety of transferrable skills.

If that's a new term for you, here's a quick explanation: Transferrable skills are gained from experience in one field and can be applied in a different field.

Your role as an admin has likely prepared you for a variety of other career paths. Depending on your skills and interests, you may be perfectly positioned to become a project manager, event planner, training coordinator, virtual assistant, database administrator, graphic designer, or HR assistant. There are countless possibilities!

Look at what you do all day and consider the aspects of your job you enjoy the most. Then, think about other fields in which you might get to do that thing you love more often.

If you know there's a specific field you're interested in pursuing in the future, use your time now wisely. Volunteer to take on "future-focused" projects—ones that will allow you to hone the specific skills necessary for your next career endeavor.

Recognize that your on-the-job experience is valuable, but depending on your area of interest, additional field-specific education may be required. For example, as an admin, you probably manage projects extensively. But, to become a formal project manager, you will likely need to obtain your PMP® certification. (Project Management Professional is a designation offered by Project Management Institute.)

In some cases, making a major career change will require a step "back" in terms of job level and possibly income. If you're an experienced administrative professional, and you want to become an event planner, for example, you may have to take an entry-level role to break into the field. While you may, technically, have experience planning events as an admin, and you may even have obtained the necessary field-specific education, you've never been an "official" event planner. You can't reasonably expect to simply walk into a high-level, high-paying role in this new field.

It is often easiest to make major career changes within an organization where you are already known and trusted. You may want to consider the opportunities that exist where you are first, before exploring other organizations.

Of course, pigeonholing can happen; this is when people in your organization simply can't or won't open their minds enough to view you as anything other than your current title. Once an admin, always an admin. This mentality can make an internal career change difficult.

Your network can also play an instrumental role in helping make your career change a reality. It is much easier for hiring managers to take a risk on someone who is new to a field when that person comes with a strong recommendation from someone the manager already trusts.

Julie Perrine (founder of All Things Admin) coined this motto for the admin field: "Start here. Go anywhere." This slogan is very appropriate. The experience you gain as an administrative professional can help prepare you for countless other roles. Used wisely, your time as an admin is never wasted.

The Choice is Yours

I believe the admin role is full of possibilities and potential. The opportunities (both within the admin field and outside of it) are abundant. But it's up to you to find, create, and seize those opportunities. They don't just magically appear without any effort on your part.

You can choose to make admin your career or you can choose to use it as a stepping stone for the future. There are no wrong paths. The most important thing is that you take your role as an admin seriously—no matter how long you expect to be in it. Try new things. Deliver even greater value. Push yourself to take on responsibilities you never would have dreamed possible. Get creative, be vocal, and take risks.

Work is like anything else in life: the more you give, the more get in return.

7

ADMINISTRATIVE LEADERSHIP

A s you learned in chapter 4, leadership is an integral part of the admin role, and it manifests in many ways. Administrative leadership can be formal or informal; it can happen inside the organization or outside. In this chapter, we'll explore these kinds of leadership opportunities and more.

Leading Without Authority

One the biggest concerns regarding leadership for admins is around lack of formal authority. As an administrative professional (in a non-managerial role), you don't technically have "power," in the traditional sense, to lead others. But that's not a deal-breaker!

In fact, leadership expert John Maxwell suggests those who leverage "position power" (based on title alone) engage in the lowest and weakest form of leadership. Maxwell further states that the more effective kind of leadership is based on the character of the individual. True, authentic leadership is when people follow someone because they *want* to—because of who that person is and what they represent—rather than simply because they *have* to.

Leading without authority requires the ability to influence. While managers and other formal leaders can direct others to do things—and impose consequences should they fail to follow through—admins must *inspire* people in more subtle ways. This doesn't mean you can't still be assertive and direct; you just can't make demands. When you're especially skilled at influencing others, you don't need to. You're able to rally people around your idea, and at times, even make them think *they* came up with it. After all, being a leader isn't about getting credit; it's about getting the job done.

Influence is largely a matter of leveraging your professional assets—namely, your relationships, reputation, and past proven results. These things earn you credibility with others. People are more willing to listen when you've already established yourself as someone whose voice is worth paying attention to.

Informal Leadership Opportunities

Admins have a near limitless opportunity to engage in "everyday leadership"—small, simple actions that help lift others and bring people together. Beyond that, I believe all support professionals must embrace leadership skills to simply execute the duties of a high-performing admin.

However, there are still more opportunities for embracing informal leadership in your role. In fact, the sky is the limit. There's no need for restraint when exploring this topic. *You have more influence than you think.* You are capable of achieving great feats of leadership within your organization—even without any formal mandate for it. You just have to approach it in the right way.

Because leadership and influence are both relatively abstract concepts, I find it most useful to discuss these topics through stories. Thankfully, in my coaching and training business, I've encountered numerous administrative professionals who have not only demonstrated exceptional aptitude for these skills, but have also achieved remarkable results because they were willing to take risks and think big.

In the following five stories, you will meet individuals who engaged in both formal and informal leadership, internally and externally. These folks weren't worried about glory or recognition; they were simply focused on helping their teams, their communities, and their organizations. When they considered how they could best do that, they didn't confine themselves to a job description. Most importantly, they were all persistent. They put in the hard work required and used their passion to keep pushing forward.

I believe each of these individuals offers a unique perspective on the topic of leadership and there is much to be learned from their different experiences.

Please note: The conversations quoted in this chapter have been lightly edited for clarity.

Barbara Cameron: Building an Enterprise-Wide Administrative Training Team

Once in a blue moon, a company gets lucky with the right person in the right position at just the right time. Barbara Cameron was that person for one very well-known, Fortune 100 global financial institution.

As the Executive Assistant for an Executive Vice President who was deeply involved in acquisitions, Barbara had a unique vantage point. In the early part of the millennium, the company was aggressively acquiring a number of banks, which meant it was simultaneously gaining hundreds of new employees overnight.

In the midst of one of these transitions, Barbara, a former public school teacher, very diplomatically approached her executive. She began by praising his efforts, acknowledging everything being done for the new employees. Then, she asked what was being done to support the assistants coming on board.

At the time, the company had no formal training program for admins. "When you were hired, they said, 'Good morning'!" Barbara laughs. "You just sat down at your desk and tried to figure out what you were supposed to do."

(For some of you, this may sound painfully familiar.)

Barbara informed her executive that the impending acquisition would bring on thirty-nine new assistants who would need to learn eleven new systems. He looked at her and said the three little words ambitious administrative professionals long to hear: *"Go fix it."*

Barbara wasted no time. She immediately put together a plan, outlining her proposed strategy for training the new assistants: Barbara, along with three fellow assistants, would physically go the acquired bank's location and sit with the new admins for their first few days, training them one-on-one in real time.

The plan was instantly approved, and Barbara and her colleagues executed beautifully.

A few years later, when another acquisition took place, Barbara and her team did the same thing again.

By the third acquisition, Barbara was an expert. This time, due to the number of employees transitioning in and the various locations involved, she had to rally twelve assistants to help her.

Upon her return, Barbara was approached by an executive leader who was blown away by her work, but curious to know why only the new assistants were getting such support. At the time, the organization had about 600 existing admins nationwide. Why not offer them training as well?

Barbara's executive enthusiastically agreed. Her trainings had been very well received, and he understood the value of expanding her work. More importantly, he also understood the massive undertaking this would be. He wanted Barbara to remain his assistant, while also leading this initiative "off the side of her desk." In other words, she was going to have another (big) job on top of her current one.

Barbara is certain, looking back, that the situation only worked because of her executive's deep commitment to the project. "I should have supported him plus at least one lower-level executive, maybe two [per company policy]. But he made it clear that, if I was going to do this, I was only supporting him."

Thus, *Admin U* was born.

Barbara started by recruiting a team of about ten fellow assistants, all of whom were passionate about the work and the organization.

"At the beginning, it was a bit of a sales job to get people on board. I talked to many executives; I knew their support was going to make or break it. I had to convince them that having their assistants involved made them look good too!"

Barbara then began building curriculum and led a train-the-trainer program for her team, teaching the basics of public speaking and group facilitation.

Before long, the team was traveling around the country, delivering training to admin groups in every part of the organization. Within the first nine months, the feedback was so positive and the demand so great, it was clear Admin U was on the right track.

In short order, the team expanded its offerings and began to organize into workstreams, based on training category, each with its own leader. While Barbara remained the overall leader of the Admin U team, she delegated many responsibilities to others, giving each workstream leader decision-making authority and the ability to fully own all aspects of their training events.

Barbara says, "I wanted to do everything myself because I had so much passion around this—*too much* passion. I learned how to let go of that because I found capable people to help."

As Admin U gained a strong internal reputation, the team received numerous requests for training and began partnering with various departments and subject matter experts to enhance its programs.

As things grew, Admin U continued to become more sophisticated and more complicated. By 2013, the team had grown to sixteen members, and they were delivering well over one hundred training classes each year for admin teams across the organization, throughout the country and at sites abroad.

In essence, it was a fully operational business division, with its own budget, management structure, and executive sponsor—but it still did not have any employees solely dedicated to it. Barbara and her team were volunteers, doing this work *in addition* to their full-time positions as assistants.

This is a big part of what made the project so difficult, but also so successful. Admin U was (and still is) "admins training admins" in the most literal sense. Its primary mission is to support the team from within, because only another admin truly understands what it takes to do this job.

Barbara remained the leader of Admin U until her retirement in 2018. At the time, the team worried the program wouldn't survive without her leadership. I had the honor of working with the group to help them navigate the transition and develop a roadmap for moving forward without their influential founder. While the process was painstaking, the team rallied together as they always have. In the years since Barbara's departure, they've found their footing, though her absence is still strongly felt.

In 2021, Admin U celebrated its eleven-year anniversary. It is a treasured and ingrained part of this organization—permanent evidence of Barbara's legacy and the impact she had. To honor her contributions, the company created the annual Visionary Award, which is granted to an assistant who takes initiative beyond the scope of his or her job and identifies a new, unexplored opportunity for their department or the organization.

For many years, word of Barbara's accomplishments has been spreading throughout the administrative community. She has received many inquiries from others who are interested in creating their own version of Admin U. To those who are up for the challenge, she offers the following advice.

Tips to Get Started

While Barbara certainly has a youthful spirit (and seemingly endless energy!) she is not shy about sharing her age.

"I was sixty years old when I started Admin U," she proudly says.

In her discussions with other admins, Barbara always reminds them that the younger generation does not have a monopoly on innovation. No matter where you are in your career, you have the power to bring new things to life, if you're willing to put in the time and effort.

That being said, it's also important to take things slowly.

"I never would have envisioned this becoming what it is—an enterprise-wide training program for admins," Barbara says. While she understood the possible scope of the project, she always took a "one step at a time" approach.

BUILDING A TEAM

Barbara believes having the right people is a critical part of success. If someone was passionate about the vision, eager to participate, and had the support of their leadership, she always found a way for them to fit into the team.

"Not everyone wants to be a trainer," she says, "and not everyone has the skills. So we developed a back office (logistics group) to handle the details. You have to have an open mind and use the talent you have on hand."

Further, Barbara emphasizes the importance of *diversity of thought*. A high-functioning team needs people with different perspectives and different ways of doing things. You need people from all generations and all backgrounds; otherwise, you run the risk of "group think," which can lead to myopic decision-making and narrow-mindedness.

As a leader, look specifically for people who challenge you. Don't surround yourself with complacent people who are just going to mindlessly agree with you. While that may be comfortable, it doesn't lead to the best outcomes.

The Importance of Strong Leadership

No matter what kind of project you're leading, as more people get involved, you are likely to experience more complexities with regard to social dynamics. This is especially true if you've built a team of strong-minded, passionate people. Without equally strong leadership, conflict can quickly erupt and hinder the team's effectiveness.

Barbara is a decisive, assertive, and compassionate leader, and these traits were absolutely necessary for the success of her program.

"This wasn't our full-time job!" says Barbara. "We barely had time to do Admin U, much less deal with drama. We needed camaraderie to make it work."

Barbara suggests the role of the leader is to help keep people focused on the mission, and, at times, make the tough calls.

"Sometimes, I would have to say, 'This isn't necessarily a democracy. We have to do it this way. If it fails, I'll put it on my shoulders. If it doesn't, we'll all celebrate as a team.'"

The Benefits

Another important point Barbara makes is that the value of a project like this extends far beyond the organization itself; in fact, everyone involved benefits. While it's a big commitment, it's also hugely rewarding, personally and professionally.

Barbara explains, "I learned to do my 'day job' quicker and better because I knew I couldn't let it falter at all. I think everyone who stayed with it became a better assistant because they *had* to."

Engaging in leadership activities will stretch your existing skills and require you to learn new ones at the same time. You're then able to apply those skills to all aspects of your job. The assistants involved in Admin U became masterful communicators, event coordinators, and organizers. They developed mentorship capabilities, enhanced their technical proficiency, and established powerful professional reputations throughout the company. These are things that will continue to benefit them for years to come.

While leadership projects require a serious investment of time, energy, and attention, the return on that investment is exponential.

These days, in retirement, Barbara is still using the skills she acquired in her admin role and in her work with Admin U to give back to her community. She continues to be a leader in every sense of the word; she participates in a variety of charitable groups and is actively involved in the lives of her six grandchildren.

Every so often, it dawns on Barbara that her career and her accomplishments with Admin U were quite extraordinary.

"I talk to my retirement community about it," she says. "I was so incredibly blessed. I went to Manila [The Philippines] and trained all of their assistants. I went to the UK, Toronto [Canada] many times, and all over the United States. I can't even tell you the number of trips I went on!"

Aside from the travel and adventure, Barbara also made lifelong friends. She and her team will be forever grateful to have worked for an organization that not only encouraged admins to get outside their comfort zone, but also supported them in pursuing and leading change. Their work has helped shape the administrative community in one of the world's most successful organizations, and it will live on for many, many years to come.

I met Barbara in 2010, just as Admin U was getting started. I knew from our first interaction that she was doing something special. I had only been training admin teams for a short time at that point, but I had already seen a lot of dysfunction within many organizations. Admins were insecure and territorial; they hoarded knowledge in an effort to make themselves feel important and protected. Of course, this behavior often backfired, but I had come to expect it.

Barbara and her team showed me what a truly high-performing admin community can do when they support one another and work together to raise the bar for everyone. Admin U is a shining example of what's possible when a smart and passionate assistant takes the lead.

Carol Walsh: Building a Community of Practice

There are many ways in which admins can support one another, and many names for such activities. Carol Walsh is following Barbara's lead and doing something similar by building a Community of Practice (CoP) for the administrative professionals in her organization, one of the largest health services providers in Canada.

In the most basic sense, a CoP is a group of people who share a profession and interact regularly for the primary purpose of learning from one another. CoPs are often informal and self-organizing. They can be an effective way to breakdown organizational silos and encourage interdepartmental knowledge-share because they often bring people together from across an entire enterprise.

CoP may be a new term for you, as it is more common in some industries than others. However, some organizations, like Carol's, actively encourage and support the creation of CoPs. In fact, the doctors and medical professionals in Carol's company have successfully used the CoP model for years. However, until Carol got involved, it hadn't been applied to the administrative staff.

"I always knew a Community of Practice to be, like, a medical journal club," Carol says. "I never thought it could be something that admins could benefit from."

Similar to Barbara's experience, Carol's undertaking started small, but quickly grew into a much bigger project.

"I supported a committee," Carol explains, "and they had a very difficult deadline with regard to minutes. They wanted them transcribed, approved, and distributed within three days. So, I had to find a way to accomplish that. Well, the chairmanship of that committee changed during the time I supported it, and when the new person came on, he was really impressed. He knew he needed to build that capacity within the admin teams across his division, so he asked me if I'd be willing to do a presentation on it."

The training was only supposed to be for about fifteen people, but the invitation kept being passed around, and ultimately, seventy-five people attended. Clearly, there was an interest!

Shortly after that, Carol got approached with another request from the same chairman *and* her own executive director. Because the chairman's division was taking on a large-scale initiative for the organization, he saw a great need to build capacity within the admin team. Carol's executive director was eager to have her involved, but she wanted to make sure her own administrative professionals would benefit as well.

"So, indirectly, that became a CoP before I even knew that's what it was," explains Carol.

To get started, Carol facilitated a focus group with the executive directors to identify skill gaps in the admin team, and then met with the admins to better understand what *they* wanted to learn.

"From that, we came up with six priority learning areas," says Carol. "Even just that awareness was valuable training. I had contacts with expertise in all of those areas from all over the organization, and I called on them to help out. The support was overwhelming. People said, 'I'd love to share what I know!'"

Over five months, the team explored a wide variety of topics including event planning, technology, and soft skills. When that wrapped up, Carol created a final report that included a clear call to action: She felt strongly that the group needed ongoing learning opportunities and managerial support for its development.

While the two executives who had authorized the project were happy with Carol's work, they were reluctant to authorize anything further at that point.

But Carol was persistent. She began to research what it would take to create an official CoP for the administrative professionals. She learned what would be involved and tried to find similar admin programs at other organizations. If possible, she wanted to adopt things that already existed, rather than recreate the wheel.

Carol then put together a charter for the CoP that outlined the proposed purpose, objectives, scope, membership responsibilities, and performance metrics for the group. Today, Carol believes this document has been a critical part of their success, because it helps keep the group focused. Without it, she says it would be much easier to get off track and take on responsibilities that are outside of their primary purpose.

While Carol was driving the initiative, she knew this had to be a group effort. So, she recruited a handful of other administrative professionals to join the Core Committee of the CoP.

"I looked for people who displayed passion for continued learning and for the importance of building capacity within our teams," says Carol.

Once they were clear on the CoP's goals, they presented the concept to the leadership team to get its support.

"It was the scariest thing ever!" says Carol. "But I had a presentation that was very well laid out, telling them what we're doing and why we're doing it, and we received their endorsement."

In fact, the leaders were so supportive, they appointed some of their own admins to the Core Committee, and today it has grown to twelve members over eight divisions. The Core Committee is responsible for identifying the needs of the group and facilitating learning opportunities—either using their own skills or by leveraging their contacts. The CoP has no budget, and therefore must use in-house resources to make things happen.

Carol admits she struggles at times because people still rely on her to be "the leader." She wants to get more people involved, and works hard to bring new voices to the conversation.

"Our true measure of success will be in how many admins become a part of this and lead parts of the work," says Carol. "The more people who know how to do the work of a CoP, the longer it will sustain itself. I imagine a group where we are all able to do the work, and we step in and out of roles and support each other as things evolve."

Ultimately, Carol and her team want the CoP to be a *group* experience.

"The goal is to create a space where the admins can say, 'I'm having trouble with this. Can you help me?' And if that trouble is happening in more than one place, we do a deeper dive and try to see if it's something that would benefit everyone. But we do still provide a lot of one-on-one support."

The CoP Core Committee has also identified four major projects to undertake, and has assigned project groups to work on them. They are:

1. Building a standardized "new hire" orientation for admins
2. Providing skills testing and learning assessments to identify gaps and help hire more effectively
3. Creating an administrative certification program, including extensive soft skills training
4. Developing an overall competency framework for the administrative role to help better align development activities

"These are long-term jobs," says Carol, "but the purpose of these project groups right now is to show leadership we mean business, and we want to put into place the things we need to support each other."

Looking into the future, Carol expects the CoP will continue to grow and attract more members from across the organization. Recently, the CoP celebrated its one-year anniversary and about 40 percent of the administrative staff are currently members.

Carol hopes the CoP will help establish a consistent standard of performance within the team and create more opportunities for those in the role. She also believes it will help elevate perceptions by showing their colleagues that admins are, indeed, professionals with their own areas of expertise—just like the medical professionals and other experts with CoPs throughout the organization.

"The goal is really: Let's learn from each other and together we can make good things happen," Carol says.

That's a simple but powerful message. Admin teams have so much to gain from supporting one another. The CoP model is another way to make that happen.

Deborah Green: Advocating for Change

Deborah Green is one more example of administrative leadership in action. As a C-Suite Executive Assistant, she helped her organization (NI in Austin, Texas) become known as an "employer of choice" among top administrative professionals. With her unparalleled passion for the profession and tenacious spirit, Deborah's work created a transformational change within the culture of NI and its administrative community.

When Deborah was hired in 2017, her executive made a request: He wanted her to evaluate how the organization was utilizing its admin staff and make some recommendations for improvement. Leveraging her twenty+ years in the administrative field, Deborah got to work right away.

Immediately, she understood the challenge in front of her. While she saw great opportunity to modernize the support role, up-level performance standards, and create more consistency within the team, she also understood the broader implications of what she wanted to do. To develop, attract, and retain a world-class admin team, the organization would need to overhaul nearly every aspect of how it was managing the administrative function.

The problem, as Deborah saw it, was multifaceted. The admin role lacked clarity of scope. Those in it were not being challenged, and the people who wanted to grow did not have the resources to do so. Overall, the value of the position was not being demonstrated, and this was reflected both in pay and in the leadership mentality toward support staff. A vicious cycle was taking place, resulting in a no-win situation for admins, executives, and the organization as a whole.

To address these issues, Deborah worked in collaboration with HR and executive leaders. She advocated for (and ultimately achieved) a number of critical changes, including but not limited to:

- Defining three distinct levels of administrative support, each with its own set of competencies, responsibilities, and performance expectations
- Establishing recommended executive/admin ratios for each level of support, which required hiring to attain
- Adjusting compensation for admin roles to be more aligned with the market and industry standards
- Providing greater support for professional development and career growth within the admin community to equip them for higher performance

These changes didn't happen overnight. They required a lot of patience and hard work; a true culture shift needed to take place within the entire enterprise. Deborah conducted in-depth research, both inside the organization and within the broader market, and gathered extensive data to support her recommendations. Her proposed changes required management approvals and considerable financial resources— she was asking the organization to *invest* in the admin community, and she needed to prove that investment worthwhile.

Deborah is humble in explaining her role in this undertaking; while she led the charge, she believes it was a collaborative effort. When asked to define some of the key elements that made success possible, she offers the following.

SEEK EXECUTIVE SPONSORSHIP

Above anything, Deborah insists that to make any large-scale change, you need the support of executive-level leadership. Find someone who deeply believes in you and your vision, and is willing to help guide you and open doors when needed.

EMBRACE INCREMENTAL CHANGE

Interestingly, Deborah was a new employee when she embarked on this project. While she quickly identified the changes she wanted to make, she had to intentionally slow down to ensure she was not alienating her colleagues.

"I had to bring people along and help them be part of the process," she says. "I knew I wouldn't be successful if I didn't get the right players involved. I had to build trusted partnerships; that was the very first step."

When you have a big idea, you need a strong personal brand to get people on board. Sometimes, it's easy to get excited and forget this part, but it's the foundation upon which you are building. Though she had joined NI with a well-established reputation, Deborah understood she still had to prove herself in this new environment.

Additionally, she had to take small wins where she could get them. In most organizations, big changes don't happen all at once. Even a small step in the right direction can still create momentum. As people began to see positive results from Deborah's efforts, her work gained widespread support, and she was able to do more at a faster rate.

THE VALUE OF COMMUNICATION

It's not enough to simply know what needs to happen; you have to articulate it in the right way. Deborah is a masterful communicator. She is persuasive and professional, clear and concise. When it comes to advocating for change, she believes an assertive approach will serve you best.

"You have to be able to *sell* it," says Deborah.

She admits her proposed changes were not necessarily brand new ideas—she was just more strategic in her approach.

"When you're asking for something this big, you have to be pretty confident," she says.

Deborah suggests focusing on organizational impact. By implementing your ideas, what might be possible for the company? What would that mean for its leaders? If your ideas were not implemented, what would the organization stand to lose? Make sure everyone you speak to understands the high stakes involved.

Leaders Must be Role Models

When you take the lead on a project like this, you can quickly find yourself in the spotlight. Deborah was trying to change perceptions about administrative professionals. She was encouraging executives to view their assistants as partners (which was a major mental shift for some) and she knew her own partnership would be on display. Likewise, she was encouraging admins to step into greater responsibility and elevate performance. So clearly, her own performance would be put under a microscope.

"You have to showcase what it looks like," says Deborah, "and exemplify the things you're trying to achieve."

Indeed, Deborah's partnership with her executive is very strong, and it serves as an example for others in the company. Deborah is careful to uphold the same level of performance for which she advocates within the admin team, and demonstrates the same qualities she promotes.

If you want to be a change advocate, understand that people will be watching you. They want to see if you "walk your talk." Just as Gandhi so famously said, you have to *be* the change you want to see.

Demonstrate Conviction

As Deborah was ushering in these major changes for the admin community, she was also supporting a C-level executive (who, incidentally, was recently promoted to CEO). How was she leading this passion project while, at the same time, managing her day-to-day responsibilities?

"It wasn't easy!" she says. "But for me it's very deep. I started in this profession when I was sixteen years old. It literally changed the trajectory of my life. So, I vowed at a very young age, if I was ever in a position of leadership, I would give back. That's where the passion comes from. If you don't have that, it's very hard to do something like this."

Administrative leadership is taxing. It's a labor of love that requires an extreme commitment of time, energy, and attention. The best way to make it happen is if you're motivated by something internal that goes beyond the goal itself.

For NI, Deborah's work has had a profound impact. In just a few years, the company has experienced a monumental shift within its administrative community. The team now feels empowered and enthusiastic about the future. Executives are recognizing the value of a high-performing admin team, and are eager to leverage their support staff at an even deeper level moving forward.

In the community, NI has gained a reputation for being a workplace of choice for top administrative professionals. Openings are highly competitive. Deborah works collaboratively with HR to handle recruiting, and while it's hard to get in, the high standards help ensure new admins are a match for the culture.

Perhaps you've noticed a theme between these first three stories: The administrative function, in many companies, is disorganized and under-supported. People on the inside—*who are actually doing the work*—are often in the best position to change that.

Michelle A: Transitioning to Management & Career Crafting

So far, we've explored stories from admins who embraced leadership in an informal capacity; they did not necessarily have any "official" leadership authority bestowed on them. They simply had a mission and motivation, and they found a way to make it happen.

There are, of course, other types of leadership opportunities for administrative professionals, including those that involve formal responsibilities, such as management.

A former coaching client of mine, Michelle A., has experienced this firsthand. Michelle works for a highly respected credit union with deep ties to its community in San Antonio, Texas. In recent years, the organization has gone through a number of major transformations, both in culture and leadership. These changes not only challenged Michelle to embrace and expand her own leadership capabilities, but ultimately helped shape the course of her entire career.

Michelle was originally hired in 2007, as the Executive Assistant to the CEO of the credit union. As part of her role, Michelle was also responsible for supporting the Board of Directors, and she quickly discovered a passion for the world of corporate governance. As the most senior EA in the organization, Michelle also supervised a team of two administrative assistants, which she found challenging but not overly grueling.

Then, in 2015, everything changed. Michelle's executive—the top officer in the credit union—announced his retirement, and the board was tasked with hiring a new CEO. This monumental undertaking required a massive amount of work on the part of every board member, and Michelle was there supporting them at every step. She was a knowledgeable guide, a trusted advisor, and respected liaison. In her support capacity, Michelle methodically led the board through the complicated, time-consuming hiring process, and in November of that year, a new CEO was welcomed into the organization.

Immediately, Michelle understood that the new CEO represented a dramatic departure from the previous style of leadership. Others recognized it too. It became clear that the credit union was destined for modernization—a prospect that excited some and worried others.

As is common with any major change in leadership, the organization experienced a wave of employee transition at all levels, and Michelle found herself in search of a new administrative support team. The admin function had long been understaffed, and with the heightened demands of the new executive leadership team, Michelle was looking for people who not only had exceptional support skills, but were also the right "fit" for the new organizational culture.

At this point, Michelle was overloaded. She was still learning how to support her new executive, putting in twelve-hour days and frequently spending Saturdays at the office. This is when Michelle and I started working together; I remember being instantly impressed with all she and her organization had been through in the previous two years. It was not surprising to me that Michelle was on the edge of burnout—and it was my job to help her avoid that.

In our time working together, Michelle hired a new executive support team, composed of two talented and motivated individuals she affectionately refers to as "lightning strikes."

"Not only did I get the culture fit, but they had amazing skillsets as well," says Michelle. "The biggest thing I had to do was just stay out of their way!"

Michelle is being modest here and generously acknowledging the innate talents of her team. In reality, her leadership was crucial as this new support group took shape, and her CEO understood this. He added "Director of Executive Administration" to her title and began involving Michelle more deeply in senior leadership discussions. After all, as a director, Michelle was now an official part of the executive team. While he had valued her contributions before, he wanted to give her a formal seat at the table.

As her team settled in, the pace of work began to even out, and Michelle turned her focus once again to governance. Through the CEO search process, her expertise had deepened tremendously, just as her relationships with the board members had. She was looking forward to turning her attention back to some important projects she had placed on the back-burner years before.

Michelle had always been forthright with her executive about her passion. He knew working with the board was her favorite part of the job—and he believed her experience with the board was an enormous asset for him, as the new CEO, and for the organization as a whole.

By the end of 2018, Michelle knew she needed more time to focus on board-related activities, and she also felt one of the assistants on her team was ready for a bigger challenge. Together with her CEO, Michelle developed a new role for herself—*Board Counsel*—a title that reflects the unique advisory position she's informally held with the board members for years. At the same time, Michelle's team member was promoted to support the CEO and manage the rest of the executive support team. Thanks to Michelle's mentorship, the transition was nearly seamless.

As discussed in chapter 3, I truly believe in the art of "career crafting," which means constructing the career you want by identifying your passions and finding ways to engage with them in the workplace. Michelle is a beautiful example of how career crafting really works.

"Obviously, governance is not everybody's cup of tea!" says Michelle. "I just have a knack for it and I really enjoy it."

Now, because of her leadership with the board, her admin team, and the entire executive team, Michelle has created a career opportunity where she gets to do what she enjoys most every single day.

While Michelle is not in a formal management role for the moment, she will be again soon. She has been authorized to build out her governance team and will be hiring an assistant to support her in the near future. She says she is hoping to find another "lightning strike."

Meanwhile, Michelle is getting more comfortable with her position as an executive leader in the organization, and she's back in a better place after teetering on the edge of burnout just a few years ago.

"I have the trifecta of employment," Michelle explains. "I believe wholeheartedly in what my organization does. I love who I work for, and I love who I work with. I have enough job experience to know that doesn't happen very often."

Indeed, this kind of ideal scenario is rare, but Michelle proves it is possible. There's a lot to learn from her story. So, for those who are looking to step into a more formal leadership and/or managerial role, Michelle offers the following advice.

THE DIFFERENCE BETWEEN MANAGEMENT AND LEADERSHIP

Michelle is a very process-driven person, which is part of what made her an excellent executive assistant. But, as her career progressed, she had to shift her perspective a bit. Michelle says she quickly learned that management is different from leadership; you manage processes, but you lead people. Transitioning from an EA to a manager required a whole new way of thinking.

Michelle explains it like this: "You have to go from focusing solely on your to-do list and what your executive is asking of you—and now you have to be higher up in your viewpoint. You have to be looking at the team, and the dynamics, and you have to be able to gauge the individuals on your team.

"That can be a challenge for somebody with my tendencies, where I'm very list-driven and I get buried in my work. But you have to be able to keep that perspective and be aware of what your team is doing—especially with an EA team because they're off supporting other executives. You might not always see their day-to-day work since you're not right there with them. You have to talk to them and to their executives frequently."

Additionally, Michelle emphasizes the importance of releasing control and allowing your team to have independence.

"I had to learn how to let go of my needs and how I think things should be done. I had to focus on whether they achieved the objective that was being asked for. I'm not saying that there aren't times when that [the strategy for getting things done] is important, and you do have to give that feedback. But I had to recognize when it wasn't important."

CONQUER IMPOSTER SYNDROME

As an EA who slowly transitioned into a formal leadership role, Michelle experienced a lot of self-doubt.

"I would wonder, 'How did I get here and who am I to tell you how to do things?'"

Psychologists suggest this kind of negative self-talk is perfectly normal, especially for high-achievers, and it's commonly referred to as "imposter syndrome."

Sitting in leadership meetings—first as Executive Assistant to the CEO, then as Director of Executive Administration, and now as Board Counsel—Michelle has always felt a little out-of-sorts. But now, she recognizes this as self-sabotage.

"I'm not a C-level executive, but I'm sitting at a table with them," she says. "But I have the most amazing boss and an amazing team of executives. *I was my biggest stumbling block* because I think they always viewed me as a member of the team. I was the one struggling with identifying myself as important enough to have a voice at that table."

Michelle also notes that her discomfort was largely related to conversations that went beyond her immediate area of expertise.

"You want to talk about the board? I'm your gal!" she says. "I can speak with absolute confidence. But over time, I started finding my voice on smaller initiatives that were being discussed too. As I got more comfortable in those exchanges, it's led me to be able to voice my opinion on almost anything."

Hire for Fit vs. Skill

Michelle attributes much of her success to the admin team she built over the past few years. As she begins the process of building her own team again, she reflects on what made the previous one so effective.

"We make each other better," she says. "It's purposeful and intentional, but it's also who we have on the team. We don't choose to tear each other down; we build each other up."

Surrounding yourself with the right people is critical. Michelle believes it's far more important to hire for fit rather than for skill. The reason? Skills are teachable. If you have someone who is willing and able to learn, you can help them develop whatever skills they need to be successful. But things like work ethic, attitude, and personality are mostly fixed traits—they can adapt somewhat, but they can't be taught. These are the qualities that determine how well a person fits within your existing team and your organization's culture.

Once in a while, you get lucky (like Michelle) and find "lightning strikes"—people who have both fit and skill. But it's unusual.

According to Michelle, being a leader also means you have to make the tough decisions, for example, when someone *isn't* the right fit.

"The way we say it is, 'Problems don't age well, and they don't transfer.' So you don't just move somebody to a different department, you—very respectfully—acknowledge the fact that they're not fitting in with the organization and you want to help them be successful and help them find their next step—but it might not be here at this company."

SHAPE YOUR ROLE

A story like Michelle's can be very exciting, especially for an admin who wants to try a little career crafting of their own. For those who are interested, Michelle offers the following advice.

"Number one: vocalize it. If you have a skill you really love and you feel like you can contribute to the organization's success by tapping into that, let people know. Secondly, ask for opportunities where you can demonstrate that skill more.

"I was really privileged to have had opportunities where I could demonstrate my skills [in governance] and it just so happened that, in my company, this particular area had a little bit of a void. But you also have to work really hard. My being able to craft this role didn't happen overnight; it was a journey of proving myself, developing trust, seeking out opportunities, and building relationships."

Focus on Self-Development

Aside from being a great example of administrative leadership, Michelle is also a committed lifelong learner. She is self-aware and willing to put in the hard work required for self-improvement. As a coach, I couldn't ask for a better client.

Even at this climactic point in her career, Michelle is still focused on continued growth, especially with regard to her management and leadership skills. She believes that, in order to effectively develop others, you first have to develop yourself.

Not surprisingly, her CEO believes this as well. He is a passionate advocate for employee development and has built an organizational culture that encourages and supports personal improvement.

In fact, this CEO has always been one of Michelle's biggest champions. The two have developed a profound bond, and it started even before the CEO joined the organization. After all, Michelle guided the board through his hiring process, so he was able to immediately experience the value of her work firsthand.

In my own dealings with this CEO, I found him authentic and unequivocal in his admiration and appreciation of Michelle's talents. I believe he saw her leadership potential even before she fully recognized it in herself.

"He's almost a little scary with his intuition," Michelle jokes.

Still, she knows that support from others is not enough. People can believe in you and want something for you, but it's all about what *you* choose to do with that. You have to take action and have faith in yourself too—which is sometimes the hardest part. But ultimately, no one else can make it happen.

"I didn't wake up one morning and decide I wanted to be a manager," says Michelle. "As an admin, it's an evolutionary process. As you develop trust with your leaders, you become a confidant, an advisor. You can influence decisions. And once you start realizing you can be a part of the things that impact your organization, you want to be a part of that *more*—especially if you really believe in what you're doing and your organization's mission like I do. I care about this organization. I want it to be successful, and I want to be a part of the process that gets it there."

Michelle often wonders if she's just lucky and if her circumstances are rare. Perhaps there aren't many CEOs out there like hers. Perhaps the vast majority of admins don't have access to the same opportunities she's had.

I argue that, yes, Michelle's organization and her leaders are exceptional. She is, indeed, lucky. But, as Thomas Jefferson famously suggested, luck and hard work tend to go hand in hand. Michelle is evidence of this. I believe there are many great organizations and supportive leaders out there. They aren't always easy to find, but they do exist.

I also believe there are many exciting career opportunities available to admins. If you're struggling to find them, follow Michelle's lead and *create* them yourself.

Ayanna Castro: Building a Personal Brand Internally and Externally

Until now, the focus of this chapter has been on *internal* administrative leadership in all its various manifestations. However, there are also many opportunities for leadership outside of your current organization, within the broader admin field. As noted previously, we are a rapidly growing global community. We need people who have unique perspectives and highly developed areas of expertise to help lead us in a positive direction. We need new and different voices to help bring more admins into the fold, and we need those who have true passion for the profession to step up and help shape its future.

This belief is what drove me, all those years ago, to create my first blog for EAs, and it's still what drives me today. I feel a sense of responsibility to the admin community, and I want to have a say in how it evolves. If you feel the same way, please know there is room for your voice—and it is, indeed, needed. Thanks to technology, we have more opportunities than ever to get our message out to the world in a big way, and engage in meaningful conversations that have a direct impact on our profession and beyond.

Ayanna Castro is an ideal example of someone who is leading both inside her organization *and* outside of it. I first met Ayanna several years ago when she hired me to do some training for the admin team where she works. We reconnected just recently when we both were scheduled to present at the Executive Secretary Live event in London.

This was the first time I had seen Ayanna on stage, and I immediately knew she had something special. Her presentation was powerful, heartfelt, and uplifting, and everyone in the room felt it. She was actually the only presenter to get a standing ovation that day!

You might already know Ayanna from her popular weekly video chats on Facebook, which she calls, "Work Your Package Wednesdays." Or perhaps you've read one of her two books, attended her annual women's conference, or seen her speak at any number of conferences and training events around the world.

But, in case you're not yet familiar with her, let's back up a bit.

From the earliest days of her career, Ayanna knew she wanted to help people. In fact, she initially went into the field of social work. However, after experiencing the emotional burnout common in such work, she transitioned to the admin field, where she quickly realized she could not only help people, but also leverage a wide range of other talents she was eager to use.

She held administrative roles at a PR firm, a college, and a private equity firm, before landing at her current company, where she has now been for over eleven years. In each role, Ayanna found opportunities for growth. Whether sharpening her creative problem-solving skills, managing complicated projects with cross-functional teams, or overseeing large-scale, million-dollar-budget events, she never backed away from a challenge.

She also never missed an opportunity for education. After obtaining her CAP, OM certification, Ayanna began to consider ongoing training and development a professional *necessity*.

Over the years, Ayanna's career naturally evolved. While she continued to grow her skills and take on new responsibilities, she was also building a powerful personal brand inside her organization.

As a senior admin supporting some of the highest ranking people in the company, she had become known as an informal employee advocate—someone with whom coworkers felt comfortable sharing their experiences. They knew Ayanna had the right reputation to make things happen and the necessary skills to get things done, and they trusted her to maintain their confidence in the process.

This informal position gave way to a formal one, when her title was officially changed to Employee Engagement Specialist in 2021. In this role, Ayanna manages projects that directly impact the employee experience—things like recognition programs, service awards, appreciation events, and volunteerism. She is now a certified PMP and chair of the Diversity & Inclusion committee within in her 1700-employee organization.

As Ayanna's career and brand were flourishing inside the organization, she was also gaining more attention externally as well. Her story is powerful—not just professionally, but personally—and Ayanna is an eloquent, engaging speaker. She has grown a large and loyal online following through her regular social media posts and videos, and has become an in-demand presenter within the admin community and beyond.

"So many admins sell themselves short," Ayanna says. "I want to be that voice to say, 'Hey, I see you, and you're doing extraordinary things! And I'm going to encourage you to *keep* doing extraordinary things.' I'm going to do that by authentically sharing my story, and hoping that it resonates with somebody."

And it definitely does.

If you have a message of your own to get out there, and you want to build a strong brand internally and externally, Ayanna is a great example of what's possible. Here's some of her advice.

FOLLOW YOUR SKILLS & TALENTS

Considering her transition from administration to employee engagement, Ayanna says, "This is the trajectory my career was supposed to go in. I just paid attention. I think your talents and your skills speak to you, and show you which way you're supposed to go."

Ayanna built her brand around her passions—helping people and managing projects. As an admin, she sought out opportunities to use her skills and demonstrate these passions, not because she had some grand plan in mind, but because that's just who she is. It was natural, and she was good at it! So the more she did these things, the more opportunities she got.

As a career coach, I often advise people to watch for these kinds of clues. When you're not sure what direction your career should go, your inner wisdom will often guide you. When you're on the right path, things will often just fall seamlessly into place (though that doesn't mean effort isn't still required!).

"Don't limit yourself based on what you're doing currently," Ayanna says. "There's no reason you can't succeed at doing what it is you're passionate about. *Be great where you are right now and everything else will keep coming.*"

LEAD WITH AUTHENTICITY

As Ayanna so simply puts it, "You can't be anybody else but yourself."

If you want to build a brand, whether inside or outside of your organization, it has to be *the real you.*

At work, Ayanna is the same person you see on social media. She believes the best way to relate to others is through honesty.

"I have no problem telling people where I started and how it laid the foundation for me to get where I am now. I don't think there are a lot of people who are willing to be transparent about *the journey.* They want to talk about the things they've done. But how did you get there? What internal struggles did you deal with?"

In her weekly Facebook videos, you may see Ayanna in her car, on her way to work, or with her kids. She's not shy about sharing the reality of her life—her own challenges and how she faces them with grace, humility, and humor.

That kind of transparency can be uncomfortable too. After all, putting yourself "out there" publicly means you're on display for the world, which can bring insecurities to the surface. Ayanna admits that, yes, she's experienced that nagging voice of self-doubt, but she is able to counter it by remembering something her grandmother said.

"She'd say, 'Don't live your life in vain.' I try my best to give honor to the life I've been given by being as authentic as possible. If one person is impacted, it will be worth it. That's how I approach everything."

CONSISTENCY IS KEY

Ayanna also believes consistency is essential to building a strong brand. That's why she's done "Work Your Package Wednesdays" nearly every week since 2017.

At work, consistency is just as important.

"Show up the same way every day," she says. "It's not just about what you do, but how you do it and how you look doing it."

Your brand is visible in everything you do—from how you present yourself to your words and your actions—and Ayanna stresses the importance of congruence.

"If people aspire to move up in their organization and want to be included in 'those rooms,' they have to look the part *and* act the part."

Navigate the Two Worlds

For those looking to build a brand within the broader admin community, it's important to think carefully about the division between your "day job" and your other activities. Ayanna is still working full time, even as she is building an active social media presence and a thriving speaking business for herself. However, she takes her responsibility to her employer seriously.

In her videos, Ayanna is always mindful to acknowledge that she's not on company time—she's either on a break or taking lunch, for example.

When sharing stories from her life and work, Ayanna is intentionally vague.

"Never say anything negative about your employer," Ayanna says. "I try to give analogies and examples to share my stories without ever disparaging the organization I work for."

Additionally, she says, "Don't use their resources for your own personal gain."

Whether it's the company computer or company time, be respectful and keep a professional separation. It's also important to avoid conflicts of interest; you probably don't want to "promote" your outside activities to your colleagues. (It's important to note here that, depending on the organization, you may be required to disclose your activities to the appropriate department, but that's different from promotion.)

Looking at Ayanna's career and side business, it's clear to see her hard work is paying off. She has built a solid brand and is now enjoying the rewards—and there are likely many more to come in her future!

It is my hope that this chapter has not only inspired you, but given you practical steps to embrace your role as a leader. Whether or not you're interested in pursuing *formal* leadership opportunities, there are countless ways in which you can demonstrate these skills, and in doing so, contribute even more to your team, your organization, and the global admin community.

8

THE COMPENSATION CONUNDRUM

B race yourself. We're entering dangerous territory.

Compensation is a hot button topic for good reason. After all, work is a means of survival for most of us. The majority of people would not do the *exact* same work in the *exact* same way if not for the financial need. If you happened to win the lotto tomorrow, or receive a massive inheritance from an uncle you never knew you had, I'm betting your career choices would change.

And let me be clear: There's nothing wrong with that! People often worry that acknowledging the fact that pay matters is somehow shallow or greedy. Nothing could be further from the truth. You're not volunteering your time and expertise here. Pay is important. Of course, it's not the *only* important thing we get out of work, but we'll talk more about that later (in chapter 10).

Pay is not a reflection of your worth as a person. Too often, people tie salary to something much bigger: a high salary inflates the ego, while a low salary creates self-doubt.

In theory, your paycheck *should* be a reflection of the value you bring to your organization. However, in practice, it reflects much more than that, including but not limited to:

- Compensation policies within your organization (e.g., are raises merit-based, tenure-based, or a combination? Are there pre-defined pay bands for specific roles?)
- Budget availability
- Other forms of compensation offered outside of pay (e.g., benefits, opportunity, etc.)
- Market conditions in your area (i.e., supply and demand for your role and your skills)
- Economic conditions in your area (i.e., cost of living)
- The value your organization places on the functions of your role
- Your past experience and education, and how they impact your ability to do this job
- Your *proven* ability to create measurable impact for your organization through your work
- Your ability to negotiate

It's worthwhile noting that, according to the Center for American Progress, "Women consistently earn less than men, and the gap is wider for most women of color."

While there are certainly systemic issues of racism and sexism contributing to this outcome, it is also often attributed to the fact that women traditionally have a more difficult time assertively negotiating. To make matters worse, when they do, they are often labelled as "difficult," where men are seen as "confident."

All of these factors are what make it so hard to talk about compensation. Some of them are within your control, but a lot aren't. This is a multifaceted, nuanced topic that a lot of career advisors present in the wrong way.

There is no simple formula to tell you what you should be making. People who make blanket statements (for example, that *every* admin is underpaid) are trying to instigate an emotional reaction—and for some, it works. But in this compensation conversation, I urge you to let logic (not emotion) prevail.

There is a broad spectrum of work that falls under the admin umbrella, and a huge variance in requirements and expectations between roles. Pay ranges in the field reflect this.

For any two individuals, the case will never be the exact same. All things will never be equal. You can't compare an executive assistant supporting the CEO of a 400-person Silicon Valley tech start-up to an EA supporting the CEO at an established twenty-person design firm in Kansas City. They may both be equally amazing assistants at roughly the same "level" (on paper), but they may have entirely different jobs and skillsets. Looking back at that list of factors impacting compensation, you would probably find many more dissimilarities between the two. It would not be unreasonable (or unfair) to expect that the Silicon Valley EA is earning *much* more than the Kansas City one.

That being said, there is a reoccurring theme throughout the business world: Administrative work has, for a long time, been undervalued. As the role continues to evolve, so must the pay scale. Some organizations have been ahead of this curve, and others have lagged behind. Again, there are a large number of factors that influence the rate of change in any organization.

When evaluating your own compensation situation, I suggest you approach it strategically. Look at it from all sides, not just your own narrow point-of-view, and apply your common sense. Recognize that a lot goes into salary decisions; it's never as clear-cut as it may appear on the surface. Advocate for yourself (in the right way, as described in this chapter), and be reasonable in your expectations. Don't make demands or give ultimatums.

A lot of people get fired up about this topic, but fiery passion is not what you need when you walk into a crucial conversation about money. You need a level head and clear plan.

Know What You Want

Whenever you're exploring compensation questions, the first step is always research. Websites like payscale.com and salary.com are useful for understanding the *general* salary expectations.

Most salary websites provide a range—based on geographical area, title, and industry—that looks like a bell curve. The majority of people earn something close to the middle amount, and fewer people earn the amounts extended to each side (more or less). It is assumed that the newer, less experienced, and/or low performing employees fall at the lower end of the bell curve while the more experienced, longer-term, higher-performing employees fall at the higher end. That means everyone else should land somewhere in the middle.

Based on your contributions, experience, tenure, and past performance, determine where you believe you should fall on the bell curve. Then, look at your current salary and calculate the percentage difference.

For reference, the US Bureau of Labor Statistics indicates that the average raise in 2018 was between 2.5 and 3.1 percent of annual salary. These numbers encompass private industry as well as government workers, and include all types of raises, whether based on a cost-of-living adjustment, performance, tenure, or anything else. Research from the Society for Human Resource Management for that same time period states that high performers earned higher than the average salary increases, around 4.1 percent. According to the research, higher raises (of approximately 7 to 8 percent) generally occur with promotions and/or job changes.

Anecdotally, I can tell you my experience confirms these numbers are *generally* accurate. I have, on occasion, witnessed situations that were outside the norm (or "outliers" as statisticians would say). I have seen people negotiate raises above 10 percent (*well* above, in some cases) and others who have literally doubled their income simply by moving to a new organization (doing the same job). However, such situations represent the exception, not the rule.

If the difference between where you are and where you want to be exceeds 10 percent of your current annual salary, it may be more reasonable to take it in incremental steps. Make a reasonable request now, and ask to create a plan to get where you'd like to be in the future.

If you choose to ask for a raise that is above the normal range, you are asking for an exceptional thing to take place. Therefore, you must have an exceptional case for why it is warranted.

What kinds of situations might justify a higher-than-average raise? Here are a few examples:

- The job description for which your salary was originally based is dramatically different from your current job description.
- Your salary is well below the market rate, or you have a competitive offer on the table from another organization.
- Your past performance has had a significant and measurable impact on the organization and is likely to continue generating a similar impact in the future.

This last bullet point is the one we'll focus on most in this chapter. After all, even if situations like the ones in the first two bullet points were to happen, performance will still impact your ability to make the raise a reality.

Know Why You Deserve It

Some raises, like those based on tenure or cost of living, have little to do with performance. Even the most mediocre performer can "earn" them. However, merit-based raises are based on what you've done, and by extension, what you are likely to do moving forward. They are both a reward for the past and an incentive for the future.

It's important to remember that piece about the future. Asking for a raise means you're asking for more money on an ongoing basis—that means there must be an ongoing return for that investment.

If you're basing a request for a raise on a project you completed that already created positive results in the past, *but is not likely to create even more positive results moving forward*, it's not a compelling argument for a raise. It might make more sense to advocate for a one-time bonus.

Alternatively, you might be able to use that project as a demonstration of your ability to do similar projects in the future, and thus generate similar results. The promise of future results, combined with proven past results, would be a better argument for a raise.

To be clear, the kind of performance that warrants a merit-based raise exceeds expectations. Emphasize work you have done that generated above average results. Ideally, you want to focus on results that others simply could not have gotten without you.

Administrative professionals often have a hard time identifying how their work creates positive results and measuring it to form real numbers. I address this topic in depth in my book, *The Invisibility Cure*, and provide numerous examples to help make the process easy. If this is an area where you struggle, you will find more support in the pages of that book.

It's worthwhile noting that, just as there are valid reasons you may deserve a raise, there are plenty of reasons why you don't.

Your personal need, for example, is not a valid reason. Your car needs a new transmission? Your kid needs braces? These things have nothing to do with your performance or your organization. They should not be discussed in any conversation that has to do with your pay.

Similarly, citing someone else's pay is never appropriate. While salaries are usually kept private, there are times when colleagues open up and talk about it with one another. Unfortunately, this can cause a major disruption. People who hold the same titles may have different salaries for a wide variety of reasons. (Refer back to the list of factors that influence compensation cited earlier in this chapter.) From the outside looking in, it's difficult to say you "deserve" a salary that is equal to that of another individual. And again, it's not a compelling argument—it's based on someone else, not you, and it's based on a perception of equity rather than on your performance.

This is especially important for administrative professionals to remember due to their access to information. In fact, not long ago, a participant in my monthly Q&A session asked a question about this. She said that, due to her admin role, she had seen payroll figures for some of her colleagues, and one in particular was earning much more than her. She wanted to know if she could use that information in advocating for a raise for herself.

My answer? Absolutely not.

As a human, I can sympathize with the desire to take this route. But as a career coach, I can tell you this approach will not go over well. The things you learn by virtue of your job—especially things related to personnel—are confidential. You can't use them as leverage for your own personal gain.

However, you *can* use the information as a mental reference point for what the organization is willing to pay for this role. You are still different people, bringing different skills and experience to the role. But you now know what's *possible,* and this may help you negotiate more assertively.

DETERMINE WHO YOU SHOULD TALK TO

In some cases, you may not be able to talk directly to the decision-maker about your request for a raise. You may have to plead your case first to the person who is your direct supervisor (such as an administrative manager). Then, that person will (hopefully) advocate on your behalf.

If you don't know who you should talk to, ask your direct supervisor. You don't want to circumvent someone in the chain of command just because you think that person might not be on your side. If that's the person you report to, it's probably the one you need to speak to, at least at first. Once you convince them, they may give you their blessing to go above or around them, but you have to follow the hierarchy. If it looks like you're going outside of the standard chain of command, you're likely to get a negative response.

I understand it can be frustrating if you're working with an intermediary and your request isn't going anywhere. A client of mine, Sandra, experienced this firsthand. Her supervisor indicated that she was onboard with Sandra's request for a raise. However, the decision-makers in HR had declined it.

Sandra wanted her supervisor to push harder for her—to really make some noise and demand the raise be granted. But the supervisor was unwilling to do so. Sadly, Sandra's request stalled out.

Sandra was, understandably, angry. As her coach, it was my job to help her see the other side of the situation. Expecting your supervisor to go to bat for you in a big way requires that person to use some of their political capital. Your supervisor might not have that capital to begin with, or this might not be the right way to use it. Perhaps the supervisor knows that, in the future, something is coming up where that capital will be needed to accomplish a more important goal. Fighting for your raise right now might ruffle the feathers of people the supervisor needs on their side for a bigger fight later. Navigating the political landscape can be delicate territory, and your supervisor isn't about to get into the gory details with you. Don't assume they don't support you just because this isn't a fight they can take on right now.

Budget constraints and pay scales might sound like a bunch of excuses, but decision makers have to work within the system. Even if they *want* to give you a raise, and even if you *deserve* it, they won't always be able to do so.

Know When to Ask

Timing is a critically important element in asking for a raise. The ideal time is during a performance review or another scheduled career conversation because, in such situations, pay is an expected topic of discussion. Some companies don't have established review periods (or they don't regularly keep to them), so it may be up to you to determine when to meet.

There are no hard-and-fast rules about timing, but there are times when you are more or less likely to be successful.

You are more likely to be successful:

- After or during a glowing performance review
- After achieving or exceeding a target goal
- After successfully completing a major project

You are less likely to be successful:

- After or during a poor performance review
- After missing a target goal or making a major mistake
- When you have a short track record (The general rule of thumb is not to ask for a major change in pay within the first year of employment, as that can suggest you accepted the job offer in bad faith—you were not happy with it and never planned to accept it for long.)

Also, consider the broader economic environment. If you know your organization is experiencing financial hardships, or if the country is in the midst of a recession, it may be more difficult to make a case for a raise.

A common question I hear has to do with layoffs. Over the years, I've worked with many admins whose companies have gone through significant downsizing, including during the pandemic. As a result, the admins had to take over a good portion of the work previously assigned to people who were let go. Because of the additional duties and increased workload, the admins felt a raise seemed warranted. But they never knew if the timing (right after a layoff) made sense.

In my experience, layoffs are pretty miserable for everyone involved. The people who remain after downsizing typically *do* have to take on more work—though it isn't always a permanent situation. In some cases, the work may be allocated differently after the dust settles a bit. Alternatively, some tasks may no longer be needed after a period of time.

The point is, if you find yourself in this situation, your workload may not be this heavy for long.

I'll refer back to the point made earlier about having a long-term track record before asking for some kind of increased compensation. If, after about six months, it appears that the new duties are intended to stay in your purview, it's appropriate to ask for a salary review. You can request your pay be adjusted to more accurately reflect the current contributions you are making.

Realize, of course, that layoffs may be due to financial turmoil, in which case, asking for a raise may sound out-of-touch or oblivious to the greater needs of the organization. Interestingly, just because a company is struggling financially (or taking proactive steps due to future concerns), doesn't mean you can't still earn a raise. It certainly happens. Budgets are allocated for different areas of the business, and your salary may fall in a category that has some room for negotiation. Plus, when the workforce has downsized, each person becomes more critical to continued operations. I've seen plenty of people get raises even in the midst of financially motivated layoffs.

If your organization's financial situation makes a raise out of the question for the foreseeable future, you may want to look at other opportunities. It's never a good sign when these things happen. While you might want to remain loyal since you were spared from the layoffs, you also have your own career to think about. Are you willing to accept this new level of work at the same pay rate for a prolonged period of time? Being severely underpaid now may make it harder to negotiate a higher salary in the future. Most hiring companies look at your current salary as an indicator of what you're willing to accept. So, think long and hard about your choices now.

SCHEDULE THE CONVERSATION

Salary discussions should never take place "on the fly." Make sure to block time off on the calendar so there aren't any interruptions, and tell the person you're speaking with generally what to expect. You don't have to be *too* specific here. You can simply say something like this: "I'd like to schedule time to discuss my performance and look at a few ideas I have for the future."

PREPARE YOUR SUPPORTING DOCUMENTATION

Never go into a salary discussion empty handed. Supporting documentation will help justify what you are asking for and why you deserve it. For example, you may gather some or all of the following:

- A list of your recent accomplishments and measurable results

- A report citing the outcomes of a big project you recently completed
- A printout of demographics that show median salary in your area for people doing the same job as you in other organizations
- Messages of praise you've received from clients, colleagues or organizational leaders
- Any recent awards you've received for your work
- Certificates for professional development you've completed

Physical evidence is powerful. While it might take some time to gather the necessary materials, it's a worthwhile investment.

Don't wait to compile this documentation until you're making a request. Be proactive and capture these kinds of things as you go. Make note of your accomplishments when they happen so you don't forget the details. Save accolades as you receive them. Keep anything that might be useful in the future and store it in an organized, easily accessible way.

Your goal is to arrive for salary discussions prepared to make your case in the most impactful way possible. Supporting documentation will add substance to your conversation.

Practice Your "Pitch"

Before you broach the salary topic with your supervisor and/or the decision-maker, talk with a trusted advisor and practice how you will make your request. Remember, if *you* don't sound convinced that you deserve what you're asking for, no one else will be convinced. Practice it over and over again until you can say it without feeling flustered, self-conscious, or embarrassed. The more you talk it through in a comfortable setting, the more confident you'll be when making your formal request.

You want this to be a positive and productive conversation; emphasize your personal pride in the work you've accomplished and your desire to continue growing with the organization. You don't want your request to appear to be motivated by unhappiness. Research suggests money is only a short-term fix for unhappy employees; most employers would rather pay a happy employee to stick around rather than try to convince an unhappy one to change his or her mind.

Also, be sure to ask for a specific number (and, of course, have a justification for it). Don't just vaguely say you want "more" money. The clearer your request, the easier it is to say yes. Plus, it shows you really thought about the situation; you're not just arbitrarily asking for more because, hey, why not?

PREPARE TO NEGOTIATE

Never go into a salary discussion with an "all or nothing" mentality. If you like your job and want to find a solution that works for everyone, you might have to be flexible. If you feel strongly that your request for a raise *must* be met—or you're willing to go find a new job—you can certainly be assertive in your discussion. *But do not make threats.* You don't want to back yourself into a corner. You might be at a tipping point, but you don't want anything to force your hand. If you're going to leave, you want it to happen on your own time.

Understand there may be certain parameters you need to simply accept. Your request may not be feasible in full, but perhaps your manager can meet you partway. Something is better than nothing. This is not necessarily the end of the conversation.

Plan to Persist

Remember that these kinds of requests may need to go through various channels of approval before they are finalized. Don't be afraid to follow up and find out where things stand.

I heard from an admin recently who said her boss mentioned giving her a raise several months ago, but then it was never brought up again. She wanted to know what to do.

The answer is simple: Ask about it! There is no potential downside in reopening the conversation. Your boss is busy and apt to forget things. That's why he or she has a support team! Your job is to help them follow through, whether that means tracking important deadlines or reminding them of the raise you talked about. More than likely, they aren't intentionally avoiding the conversation; it simply slipped their mind.

Lastly, if your request for a raise is denied altogether, don't just give up and walk away. Always make sure you understand why. Further, ask if it's possible to create a plan that will help position you for what you want in the future. What would they need to see? What would need to happen? You need to know there is at least an opportunity for financial growth in the future. Otherwise, if this is the most you can ever hope to earn at this organization, perhaps it's time to focus on your exit strategy.

KNOW WHEN TO MOVE ON

If you haven't had *any* kind of pay increase for several years, it's important to realize you are now making *less* than you were previously due to inflation.

For anyone who has gone a prolonged period of time without a raise, my question is always this: Have you asked? If not, you need to do that first, using the specific strategies discussed in this chapter.

If you have delivered exceptional over-and-beyond value, and you've asked for a raise and been denied many times over again, then it may be time to consider other opportunities—regardless of the reasons you're given or the "promises" you may be hearing about the future. Sure, budgets may be tight and rules may exist that limit what you can earn. But unless you really just love working at your organization and don't mind holding out for something to change, you're probably better off looking elsewhere.

Going five or more years without a raise creates a dangerous pattern for your career. Hiring companies always want to see that you've progressed in your previous employment, and a rising salary is one sign of progression. If you remain stagnant, that doesn't look good.

Plus, your current salary is generally seen as a "starting point" for salary negotiations with other employers. The higher you are now, the better off you'll be in the future.

Unfortunately, there is no hard-and-fast rule about how often raises should be given. You need enough time to deliver great value, and your organization needs enough time to see the impact of your work. How long that takes can vary.

You also need to consider where you are on the pay scale already and how much room you have for growth. How much do you earn as compared to your peers in similar roles and with similar qualifications? If you're already at the top of the pay range (meaning you couldn't easily go elsewhere and earn more for this work), you're likely to have a tougher time getting your raise. Thus, you may experience longer periods of pay stagnancy, which may be unavoidable.

Additionally, in my experience, large salary increases are difficult to come by. If you haven't received a significant raise in an extended period of time, and now feel your experience warrants a dramatic jump, you may need to leave your current employer to get it. That's not always the case, but it's common.

While it sounds counterintuitive, you have more leverage when you're negotiating for a new job as opposed to negotiating as an existing employee. Your current employer knows how hard it is to launch a job search. They're banking on the fact that you'll stay where you are comfortable, even if the salary isn't ideal.

However, a new employer wants to bring you in. They're willing to do what it takes to get you on board and they're more flexible about salary at the beginning of the relationship.

Simply put: If you feel you deserve a raise, ask for it and take the evidence with you to prove your case. If you want to stay where you are, it's always worth a shot, even if you know it's not likely to happen. Should your request be declined, you can then make moves to go elsewhere, knowing you did your best to make it work.

No employer should expect high-performers to stick around forever without enjoying some kind of financial growth. Further, if you end up with another offer in hand, you may be able to inspire your current organization to meet your pay requirements to keep you. Don't count on something like that, but it could happen.

Is Admin a Lucrative Career Path?

People who thrive in the admin career are those who have a passion for the work—not those who are simply driven by money. If it's a big paycheck you're after, there are plenty of other jobs where you stand to make a whole lot more. You probably won't become a millionaire working as an administrative professional. But who knows? Stock options at the right company could change that.

A high-performing admin can expect to earn a comfortable living, and those who rise to the top of field can expect a bit more. Is it a lucrative path? Well, that's relative. It depends on your point-of-view.

I started my admin career working as a secretary at a doctor's office while going to college. I earned a nice hourly wage, but I also lived like the average college student and still had significant help from my parents.

In my last admin role, as an EA at a wealth management firm, I earned a very nice living. My salary was generous, and I also received a sizable annual bonus.

There are a wide variety of perspectives on this topic. Some people will tell you there's no money to be made in this field, but I disagree. The vast majority of admins I've worked with have been generally happy with their pay situation. Of course, no one would *mind* more money, but most feel they are well compensated and have room for growth.

Pay Matters (But It's Not Everything)

I mentioned in chapter 1 that my website is EatYourCareer.com and the concept behind it is all about creating a *nourishing* professional life. I truly do believe that work can be an enriching part of the life experience and can provide value far beyond the paycheck. However, it must *first* meet your financial requirements. If you aren't paid a wage you believe is fair for the work you deliver, nothing else matters. Without this fundamental level of satisfaction, you won't ever reach the higher levels of mental, emotional, and social fulfillment.

Psychologist Abraham Maslow explored this concept and illustrated it in the Hierarchy of Needs created in 1943.

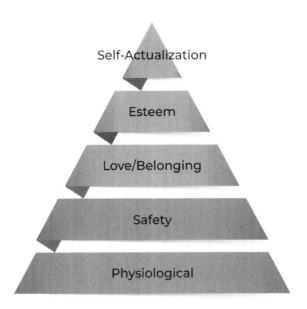

Figure 3. Maslow's Hierarchy of Needs

At the bottom of the pyramid, Maslow identifies physiological needs and safety needs—the basic requirements for survival. He believed people must have their bottom level needs met before they can become motivated to achieve higher level needs (like those associated with belonging, esteem, and self-actualization).

If we apply this model to the workplace, pay would fall in the bottom category. It helps us provide for our physiological needs, as well as our safety needs. Career nourishment is an element of self-actualization, right at the top. That's the place where we're achieving our true potential and experiencing the joys of personal growth. We only get there by first achieving everything else that falls beneath it.

Earning a satisfactory wage is the first baby step toward nourishment, so it's important—but it's not everything. Your potential for career fulfillment does not infinitely increase in direct proportion to your salary. Making more money won't necessarily make you happier at work (or in life), especially once you've already reached a certain point. Only you can determine what that point is *for you*.

When it comes to matters of pay, try to keep it in perspective.

The work you are doing is important and valuable; you deserve to be paid fairly and appropriately for it. But it's not always about you. Don't take compensation decisions personally. If you're not happy with your current situation, you have the power to change it.

In every field, you will find people who are disgruntled and pay can always contribute to their unhappiness. My belief is this: If you are not satisfied with your pay, do something about it. Advocate for a raise, get a new job or find a new career. Don't simply stay where you are, complaining about it. That's not productive or healthy for anyone.

9

ADDRESSING COMMON COMPLAINTS AND CONCERNS

As a career coach and trainer for the administrative community, I've heard it all—the good, the bad, and the ugly. Over the years, I've noticed some general patterns regarding complaints and concerns in the field.

Let's start by acknowledging a hard truth: No job is perfect; no career is without its challenges. You need to have realistic expectations. At the same time, you have to take responsibility for your own happiness.

In this chapter, I've outlined the five most common complaints and concerns I hear from administrative professionals, along with recommendations for how to address them in a productive way.

This is, by no means, an exhaustive list of the challenges you may face in the admin role. Throughout this book, I've already addressed a number of other common issues, like not having a predefined career path and lacking managerial support for professional development. I've already offered a wide array of strategies to not only address your workplace frustrations, but hopefully prevent them from happening in the first place.

Still, anyone can find themselves in an unfortunate situation at work. It is not necessarily a reflection on you as a person or as a professional. Some people just don't fit in certain roles at certain organizations. There is no shame in recognizing this and making a conscious choice to find a better fit.

No one should feel like a hostage in the workplace. You always have choices—even if they aren't the most comfortable options.

However, before you throw in the towel, I suggest you take a good look at the situation and see what you can do to improve it. I've worked with many admins who were ready to give up, but decided to work with a career coach first in an effort to turn things around. Through a process of intense self-reflection and hard work, some of these people did, indeed, resolve their issues. I'm happy to say that some experienced dramatic turnarounds!

Of course, some did not—but they made the decision to move on knowing they did everything in their power to make it work.

If you're experiencing any of these challenges, know that you're not alone. The strategies here will help you evaluate your situation and take positive steps forward.

1. There is an overall lack of respect for admins at my organization.

As discussed in chapter 2, administrative professionals are often saddled with antiquated notions about what their role is and how they contribute to the team. Sadly, some organizations have developed cultures in which admins are treated poorly and viewed as inferior. There is a prevailing sense that admins are somehow "less than."

I want to begin by reminding you that these perceptions are inaccurate, and you deserve better. My hope is that, as you grow your career, you take a discerning approach in your future job searches. Research the culture of the organizations at which you are applying. Talk to people there. Ask specifically about the perceptions of the admin community, and how the company supports its support staff. You can and will find *many* organizations that respect and appreciate their admins—but don't take it for granted. Do your homework.

If you find yourself working in an environment where admins are not respected consistently and throughout the organization, here are some things you can do to potentially improve the situation for yourself and others.

To start, realize that working long-term in a culture like this can really wear on an admin team. It is likely the admins operating in this culture have been a bit "brainwashed" for lack of a better word. They might not even see anything wrong with the situation! Many of them might not believe they actually deserve anything different.

This attitude only creates a dynamic that reinforces the bad stereotypes and inaccurate views! After all, if you're constantly looked down upon, why would you care about performing exceptionally in your role? If others don't take you seriously, why take yourself seriously? If you're treated like an unskilled worker, why bother stretching and leveraging your skills?

In my experience, this kind of culture can not only demotivate admins and reduce their effectiveness, but it can also downgrade their overall professionalism and behaviors toward one another. These are the companies where I often see admins wearing yoga pants to the office and engaging in catty, backstabbing behavior with their teammates.

If this is what people throughout the organization are seeing, what would inspire them to change their perceptions?

It's a nasty, vicious cycle that's hard to stop.

In such a situation, your only option is to focus on what you can control and what you can influence.

Namely, you can control your own behaviors—how you speak about yourself and your fellow admins, how you interact with others, and your own work performance.

Through this kind of role modeling, you can influence the rest of the admin community to "up their game." You can also influence others throughout the organization by showing them what a top-tier admin can do. Perhaps they've never experienced true administrative partnership. Maybe they don't know what it actually looks like to leverage the talents of a career-minded support professional.

I believe strongly that administrative training can also help create a cultural shift in perceptions. When admins receive company-sponsored support for their development, they feel more valued. They are inspired to see themselves in a different way. The rest of the enterprise sees this investment too, and it causes a positive ripple impact. This alone would be worth it, but training also gives the admin team a new set of tools with which to work, so they have the resources they need to perform at a higher level as well—both individually and as a collective group.

As a trainer, I have seen tremendous growth from admin teams involved in my programs. It's no exaggeration to say that entire organizations have felt the impact. This is a testament to the participants, not me. They came to training with an open mind and a willingness to do things differently. They saw training for what it was—a gift and a call to action—and they didn't squander the opportunity.

Additionally, administrative certification can be a powerful tool in shifting perceptions. One of the biggest rewards of obtaining certification is that you get to put a few small letters after your name—CAP or PACE, for example. Professionals at all levels understand that having a designation demonstrates a substantial achievement, even if they don't know exactly what the letters stand for.

When a certified admin within an organization proudly displays his or her letters in an email signature, for example, it sparks interest. People may inquire about what it means. This is an opportunity to share more about your chosen career path. Many people don't know that the admin field has its own body of knowledge, just like other professional fields. They aren't aware that career-minded admins have certification opportunities and are united within various professional associations (like IAAP and ASAP) that help set standards in the field.

Often, once a few admins obtain certification, it catches on like wildfire. Others feel a certain amount of pressure to "step up." This can be a very good thing because it helps to establish an elevated standard across the board, and that's necessary to shift the organizational culture.

Note: If you would like assistance in advocating for admin training and/or certification within your organization, please reach out to me. I'd love to help.

Remember that culture change can be a tediously long process. It's like trying to turn the Titanic. You can't move too quickly or the whole thing tips over. It often takes years for a toxic culture to develop; it won't change overnight. But steady, small adjustments can add up and before too long, you could discover you've charted a new course for the team.

Still, I would be remiss if I didn't also say that you are not solely responsible for shifting an entire organization's culture around how they view and treat admins. You can't do it on your own. You need support from others in the community and from leadership.

You also don't have to be the one to instigate change. You are always free to find a new organization where admins are already treated with the respect they deserve. Not everyone has the energy or interest in taking on this kind of leadership. It can be a hard road. It's not selfish to walk away and take care of your own needs if that's the better option for you.

2. My boss is a micromanager and isn't releasing control of things!

There's a big difference between "management" and "micromanagement." Some executives want to be more involved in the work, some less. Some are more willing to release control quicker than others. These things are not necessarily bad. It's all personal preference. It only becomes "*micro*management" when the involvement is so overbearing that it actually hinders your ability to perform fully.

Still, as an admin who wants to elevate, this can be tricky. How do you get a micromanager (or even just a heavily involved manager) to release some control and allow you to take the reins? Here are some suggestions.

First, reflect on the cause. It is *you* or is it *them*? Micromanagement and control issues generally stem from a lack of trust. Is it possible you've done something in the past to break trust or something that suggests you need a heavier amount of managerial involvement to get things done? Be honest with yourself.

Or maybe their distrust has nothing to do with you. Maybe they've had bad experiences from a past assistant or another employee, and now they have a hard time releasing control because of that.

No matter the reason, your job is to demonstrate the traits that instill confidence in your ability. If trust needs to be built or repaired, that must come first. Trust is a natural byproduct of consistent, reliable behavior. Your executive needs to know they can expect high-quality work and excellent performance from you at all times.

If you believe your performance already warrants this trust but it's not yet there, consider having a conversation. Discuss your desire to take on more responsibilities and why it's in your executive's best interest to release control to you.

Analyze it like you would an investment: Let's say your leader is spending thirty minutes per week on a report you could reasonably handle. And let's say it would take you three hours to learn how to do that particular task. Your executive would invest three hours of his or her time to train you and the return would be thirty minutes per week. Once you've done the report for six weeks, you're at a break-even point. After that, it's all profit—extra time in your executive's pocket.

This can be a compelling argument for leaders, so lay it out in black and white. Run the numbers, then ask explicitly for the trust required to make it happen. (Note: You never want to use the word "micromanagement" in such conversations. Instead, focus on your desire to provide deeper support in a more autonomous way.)

Many executives have never been trained on how to properly leverage the talents of their support staff. They need you to teach them—and in my experience, they need more than a gentle nudge. They need clear, confident instructions.

When you identify a specific task you can or should take over for your executive, speak up assertively. Say something like, "I can handle that for you," or, "Why don't you let me take over?"

Wherever you can, *assume* responsibility for admin duties. That's your job, after all. Grab anything and everything that falls under your scope of work *before* your boss can take control. The more he or she sees you're capable of handling these things without them, the more they will be willing to send your way in the future. As you demonstrate confidence, their confidence in you will grow.

It can also be helpful to start off slow and small. Rather than taking over an entire reporting process, for example, you could ask to do one piece of it. You can assure your executive you'll keep them informed every step of the way. One you've done this enough, you'll be able to check in less frequently. And, once you've proven yourself successful with that one small piece, you can take another and another. It builds from there.

Also, consider suggesting a "trial and review" period. You can take over certain things for a limited period of time—say, for thirty days. That way, if your manager isn't happy during that time, he or she can take it back. It's often easier to agree to changes that are seen as temporary. But it still gives you a chance to show what you can do. Even in just a short period of time, you may be able to create enough of a positive impact to inspire your exec to release control permanently.

Above all else, be pleasantly persistent. Your executive might hold tight to control on certain things, but with a little effort on your part, that could change in the future. Don't give up just because you heard "no" the first time around. You don't have to nag; just continue to make your case.

To illustrate this point, I'll share an example from an executive and assistant I spoke to after a training event where I presented several years ago.

The assistant had felt strongly that she needed to be involved in managing her executive's email inbox. She knew he was receiving close to a hundred messages a day, and most were falling through the cracks. The assistant wanted the ability to help organize and prioritize messages, and also respond to urgent requests on the executive's behalf.

For years, the assistant received pushback from her executive. He didn't like the idea at all! Even though he trusted his assistant, it scared him to release that level of control.

But the assistant didn't give up; she just backed up a bit. Instead of asking for the whole enchilada, she asked just for inbox visibility. If she could at least see what was happening (without actually touching anything) it would give her important context. She would be able to monitor requests and progress, and be more proactive about keeping her executive on track.

This worked! The executive opened a teeny tiny crack in the door and let her in. And the assistant was able to do a lot with it.

But she still knew she could do more. So, she would occasionally tell him how many non-actionable messages she saw cluttering his inbox. She could archive those for him—*if* she had the right permissions. She would occasionally type up

the response she would send to a certain message in his inbox
—*if* she had the ability to respond on his behalf.

Over time, little by little, she proved her point and
demonstrated she was more than capable of handling the
responsibility of greater inbox control.

While recounting this story to me, the executive told me he was
so glad she didn't give up. He needed time to get comfortable,
but she knew it would help him. And it had! He had a hard time
putting into words just how much of a relief it was to have his
assistant's support with his email. A year before, it wasn't
something he ever thought he would or could do, but when I
spoke to him, he couldn't imagine ever going back to the way
it was.

There is, of course, a point at which persistence goes from
pleasant to unpleasant. Watch for non-verbal cues that indicate
your message is not being well received, and back up if you see
them. If you've been pushing on something for a while, but
you're not feeling any progress, you can always ask, "Is there
anything I can do to convince you?" or "Would you like me to
stop pushing on this?" Ultimately, it is your leader's choice how
they leverage you. You can steer them gently in the right
direction, but you can't force them.

All of this being said, it's important to remember that a
partnership is a two-way road. You want to find someone who
has a similar vision of what this relationship is all about, and
someone who is willing to give you the opportunity to really
thrive in your role. If that's not possible where you are, it may
be smart to explore other options.

3. I'm giving too much to others, and I'm headed for burnout.

This is perhaps the most common concern I encounter with admins. The reason is pretty obvious: Admins are *support* professionals. They tend to be very *supportive* people. They are constantly focused on the needs and goals of others. Consequently, their own needs and goals often go uncared for.

To even recognize this is happening is a feat. Most don't see it until the problem consumes them. I can't tell you how many admins I've met who were actively in the midst of burnout.

To be clear: "Burnout" is a condition resulting from complete mental, physical, and emotional exhaustion, typically caused by prolonged periods of unmanaged stress. Symptoms can vary in severity and span a wide range. Some people experience intense physical problems—everything from chronic headaches to serious medical issues. Others suffer with feelings of depression, overwhelming fatigue or lack of motivation. Some simply find themselves emotionally volatile, breaking down in tears one minute followed by tremendous rage the next.

Burnout is a deeply complex and personal experience that can take months or years to recover from. In fact, many people claim to have ongoing residual effects (similar to PTSD) long after they have technically "recovered."

According to one study, more than half the people working in "high-pressure" careers will experience burnout. Of course, this is a fairly subjective classification. What is high pressure? Surgeons hold people's lives in their hands, so that definitely qualifies. But I would argue that admins can experience intense pressure too, even if it's not of the "life or death" variety. Actually, any position can *feel* high pressure.

Sadly, many admins put that pressure on themselves. They have an unrealistic idea of what they can and should be able to handle. They aren't comfortable setting limits and negotiating expectations, so they allow others to add more and more to their plate, until they're completely overloaded. They skip breaks, eat lunch at their desk, and stockpile vacation time for fear that things will fall apart without them.

This kind of self-imposed pressure is a recipe for disaster. It's also one of the reasons I really resist the "superhero" language that admins and admin supporters often use. Recently, I even saw a job opening that was titled, "Office Superhero Needed!"

You are not super human. You're amazing! You can probably make seemingly impossible things happen! But there is always a cost. You can't just endlessly take on the world without ever paying the price. Trying to live up to that superhero image is what gets us into trouble.

You have normal, natural, fully acceptable human limitations (of time, energy, and attention) that you, and others, should respect. It's your responsibility to understand your limits, express them clearly, and manage them effectively.

This is commonly referred to as, "saying no," which is yet another phrase I'm not fond of. I especially reject the old cliché, "'No' is a complete sentence." I understand it isn't meant literally, but some people take it that way.

Yes, we all need to set limits. But we can do so in a way that isn't abrupt and isn't going to immediately turn people off. In the professional world, we need to work with our team to find solutions. Saying "no" stops the conversation and generally makes others feel slighted. I tend to suggest that "no" should be reserved for times when you are being asked to do something that is unethical, illegal, or outside the scope of your authority. Otherwise, for a legitimate work request, it is far more effective to first try renegotiating or redirecting.

Here's what I mean: If someone asks you to stay late to work on a presentation, you have options. If you agree to stay late, perhaps you can earn some goodwill with that person. Maybe you can add it to the "above and beyond" list you share with your boss each month. Staying late *occasionally* is a nice way to demonstrate commitment and build some strong allies.

But, if you've stayed late for several nights in a row, or if your kid has a special event that night, or if you're just plain exhausted from the day-to-day workload you've been handling, you can always offer some other solutions. For example:

> "I'd be happy to get it started while I'm here, then I can pass it off to someone else when I leave this evening."

> "I can build a basic template, and then you could fill in the missing info on the slides."

> "I can definitely work on it tomorrow if the deadline can be pushed by a day."

Rather than simply saying "no," these options show you care about the request and want to find a way to be supportive. I understand this doesn't always work. There may be times when the request has no wiggle room. In such situations, you may have to find a way to make it work—and *occasionally*, that's okay. Or, you may have to more assertively say, "I'm sorry I'm out of options. I'm just not able to stay late tonight."

If this kind of thing happens too frequently, you need to have a conversation with your leaders, at a time when a request is not directly being made. This is about aligning expectations and defining what you need.

Expectation setting, ideally, should be done at the start of a new partnership. Get clear, upfront, about how often late nights are needed, if you're expected to check email outside of normal business hours, take phone calls, etc. You can then work together to make sure you're both comfortable and supported in the partnership.

Research shows that work stress is often directly tied to a lack of control over the work and a lack of certainty. Having these kinds of conversations can help alleviate these issues.

You may need to have these conversations on an ongoing basis. It seems that, from time to time, people's expectations change and they forget to verbalize it. If and when that happens, it's time to pause and realign.

Additionally, you may need to have regular conversations to better understand priorities. When you have a lot on your plate, you can't reasonably be expected to do it *all* right *now*. Some things must be strategically postponed. If you're not sure which things are okay to put off and which aren't, discuss it with your leaders. That's what they're there for! They have context you might not have. Just be sure you don't approach the conversation from a place of stress and overwhelm. Instead, approach it as a collaboration:

 "I'd like to get your insight on how best to allocate my resources."

Remember you are, more than likely, not working on life and death matters. If things have to wait and people can't always get exactly what they want when they want it, they will probably survive. The business will be okay. Don't put an unnecessary weight on your shoulders. You are important, but you are not responsible for carrying everyone and everything.

In fact, your most important responsibility is to yourself. If you give everything to others, there's nothing left for you. That means you'll be completely tapped out when you get home to your loved ones each night. Your weekends will be spent "recovering" rather than relaxing and enjoying life. Your world will slowly begin to shrink.

People will keep taking as long as you let them. They will push your boundaries over and over again if you don't set them and hold firm. You can't even blame them! It's *your* responsibility, not theirs.

Lastly, it's important for all admins to learn how to protect their *emotional* space as well. Too often, we allow the stress of others to become our stress. Someone else's bad day turns into ours.

I struggled with this for many years before I finally came to understand that my emotions are sacred. I should not give anyone power over them. I get to choose how I feel at any given moment of the day.

Eventually, I got to a point where I could separate my emotions from my boss's. When my executive was freaking out over something (and I use this term with love), I would offer support, I would listen, I would care—but I would not take ownership of it. The realization that I could do this was empowering and invigorating!

This kind of compassionate detachment, as I call it, is crucial for administrative professionals. We are greatly involved in the business of others. We want them to succeed and be happy. But we can't let ourselves get too deeply intertwined emotionally. We must keep a healthy, professional separation.

4. My boss is a "bully."

Before you define anyone as a bully, think hard about what you are really saying. In my estimation, this word is used far too frequently and it's not always an apt descriptor.

Instead of applying a controversial label to your boss, try to define the behavior you are seeing in more practical terms. For example, "My executive criticizes my work when there's nothing wrong with it," or, "My executive uses an aggressive tone of voice and yells at me in front of others." These are real behaviors that are, indeed, not acceptable. But, when you define the situation in real terms, you can now address the specific behaviors and possibly resolve the situation.

We teach people how to treat us by showing them what we are willing to accept. If you let your boss yell at you without addressing the situation, you've just taught him or her that it's okay. Instead, wait until the heated moment has passed and say something non-emotional and clear cut such as, "I'm not comfortable being yelled at in front of everybody. Next time a situation like this comes up, can we speak in private about it?"

The more clearly you establish your boundaries upfront, the more you will wrangle a "bully" into place. Do not allow yourself to become a victim of *anyone*—be it your boss, your coworker, or anyone else. If you do not address the behavior that is troubling, you are silently accepting it.

I also encourage assistants to develop a thick skin. Often, executives are not really bullies. They are simply intense, highly driven individuals who have high expectations for themselves and others. They are human, like all of us, and they have bad days. They may occasionally make mistakes and fall short of our expectations for them. They may snap or speak a little too harshly in the heat of the moment. Stand up for yourself, but be willing to forgive the occasional misstep.

Of course, some executives are indeed the classic definition of a bully. They may *consistently* behave in a way that is intended to frighten, degrade, or intimidate you. They may abuse their position of power in extreme and repetitive ways, creating an impossibly difficult relationship dynamic and overall work environment.

If this is the case, I recommend the following:

1. Start by clearly stating your boundaries and identifying when those boundaries are being broken.

2. Document all communication and interactions you find unacceptable.
3. Seek outside counsel from a trusted advisor or mentor. Share specifics with the person and ask for their perspective and guidance.
4. Consider involving a representative from your organization's HR department. They may be able to provide support in the way of mediation or imposing consequences for the behavior.

Let's dive into that last point a bit more, since HR has a way of dividing people. Some argue that its purpose is not to serve you, the employee, but to protect the company. Therefore, you can expect no support from them.

I don't see it that way. Yes, HR is tasked with protecting the organization from potential legal problems. But employee issues absolutely fall under that umbrella! It is in their best interest to listen to your concerns and provide assistance.

That being said, HR is *not* there to simply do whatever it is you want them to do. They have procedures and policies to follow. In almost any case, they will want to investigate allegations and that often requires gathering evidence and speaking with all the individuals involved. If you want things to "stay quiet," that's not your call. Once you involve HR, the situation is out of your hands. They are now mandated to do what they see fit, even if it's not what you want.

I find most people who don't like HR have had bad experiences because they have unrealistic expectations or they simply didn't like the outcomes of HR's involvement. That's a risk you take when you bring them in.

In my experience, bullies don't often change. While I do believe their behavior will catch up with them, there's no telling when karma will show her pretty face. You don't have to stick around waiting for it to happen. If the behavior is truly unacceptable and you've made a reasonable effort to make things work, it's time to move on.

I know that feels unfair. Why should you leave when the bully gets to stay? Think of it this way: Do you really want to work for an organization where this kind of thing happens? What does that say about the culture? Even if this situation gets miraculously resolved, what's to stop it from happening again?

Some would argue you should stay and advocate for the cultural revolution this organization needs! Stand up for your rights and the rights of others!

You are more than welcome to do that, and I applaud those who do. But that's a lot of weight to put on your shoulders. It's not necessary. You are not "running away" by leaving. You're protecting yourself. You're *freeing* yourself. Maybe others will be inspired to follow your lead, but ultimately, they are responsible for their own choices.

There are plenty of fabulous executives in great organizations who need support. Whether your boss is a bully or just someone you don't particularly like, you owe it to yourself not to settle. Life is too short to work for a jerk.

5. I'm bored and unchallenged.

One of the things I love most about the administrative role is the great diversity of work. You never know how your day will unfold. With such a wide variety of things to focus on and different people with whom to interact, I find it hard to believe so many admins express feelings of boredom.

Logically, I get it. Doing the same work, day in and day out, can get repetitive and mind-numbing—regardless of how many different things you're doing. Even the most exciting work can become monotonous when you do it enough. Anyone, in any role, can experience boredom if they aren't actively working to stay engaged and stretch their skills on a regular basis.

Think of your favorite band, for example. When you go see them in concert, chances are pretty good they'll play their most popular hit songs at every stop on the tour. They *have* to, especially for the folks who aren't hardcore fans like you. The band members are probably so sick of playing those songs! They could do it in their sleep! That's why they also have to mix things up. Some bands will add a little variation to the popular stuff; some will play songs they're still working on. Others will jam out on stage for a bit, experimenting just for the fun of it. This is how they keep things interesting for themselves and for the audience.

I firmly believe boredom is the birthplace of genius, and as poet Dorothy Parker so profoundly said, its only cure is curiosity. When people get bored, they have two options: allow that tedious, tiring state to wash over you and fill you with a quiet misery, or look for ways to jazz things up—get creative and make your own magic!

Just like your favorite band, you still need to deliver the "hits." Those things you could do in your sleep? Yep, they're part of the job. But maybe you can improve upon them. Perhaps you can challenge yourself to find new, better, or faster ways to do them. Maybe you can track some stats associated with the work and set a goal to beat your "score" by a certain amount each time or create a friendly competition with your colleagues. Who knows what efficiencies you might find?

Beyond that, I also encourage you to look for and create opportunities to get involved in different kinds of activities.

Ideally, you're looking for projects that:

- Interest you
- Leverage your current skills
- Allow you to build new (desirable) skills
- Provide value to the organization

That last bullet point is especially important. The goal is not simply to entertain yourself or develop your skills on company time. Sure, these things might be side benefits. But the primary purpose needs to be focused on the organization.

Here's an example of the kind of thing I'm suggesting.

As an executive assistant, I worked on a lot of client communication projects, but I knew I wanted to hone my writing skills even more. My day-to-day work had become quite routine, and I was feeling the early stages of boredom setting in.

One day, my boss off-handedly mentioned the idea of starting a client newsletter and I latched on to it!

Within a few days, I had taught myself MS Publisher and created a sample template of what our newsletter might look like. When I showed my boss, he was thrilled and told me to keep going. I wrote up a few articles, asked others in the office to do the same, and suddenly, I was in charge of a major, high-profile, high-impact project.

Looking back, I remember the early days of working on that newsletter as some of the most exciting in my admin career. I can also say the successful launch of the newsletter and the ongoing operations I implemented to maintain it were some of my greatest achievements. But beyond that, my work had a measurable, positive effect on the organization. It was a win-win.

In my experience, boredom is rarely a continuous state; it tends to ebb and flow. Most organizations have a natural rhythm. There will probably always be periods when things are hopping and you simply don't have time to get bored. Then, things will slow to a crawl and you'll encounter feelings of restlessness again.

For this reason, I also find it useful to keep a list of little pet projects that aren't urgent but would be "nice to do" at some point. We all have these things, and it's likely your leaders do as well. They may mention them off-handedly (like my former boss did) or you can specifically inquire about them. Capture these ideas, so when the early signs of boredom start appearing, you can pull out your list, select a project and get moving.

For example, some things that might land on this list include:

- Create or update a procedures binder where you outline the step-by-step processes for completing all of your most critical tasks
- Create or update preference profiles for each of the people you support
- Reorganize your paper or electronic files and purge old or out-of-date documents
- Reorganize/clean out your physical workspace
- Explore a new software
- Engage in professional development activities
- Upgrade the look and feel of templates you use frequently (like PowerPoint slides, Word documents, etc.)
- Map out an existing process and look for ways to make it more efficient and improve outcomes (Take note of specific processes that would benefit from such analysis)

This list is just the beginning! You may be surprised by how long it can get.

While I recognize boredom is a normal reaction to routine, I also strongly advise you to be wary of it. Allowing yourself to stew in it for too long can have dire consequences. From the outside, it will make you appear disengaged and demotivated, and it can drag down others around you.

Remember, like most of the things discussed in this chapter, it's your responsibility to find a way out of it. Don't simply tell your boss you're bored or you want "more" to do. That's just adding another task on his or her plate. It's putting the onus on them, and they won't appreciate it. Instead, bring ideas! Offer ways in which you can contribute more to the team. This will shift the conversation to a much more positive, productive place.

Challenges come up in any job. I don't think the admin role has a disproportionate amount of them. However, I do think admins often look to others to solve their problems when it's not necessary. You have more power than you might think! The key is to address your challenges head on and implement tried and true strategies like the ones discussed in this chapter.

If you are struggling to deal with things on your own and you'd like some more direct support, you may want to consider working with a career coach or seeking guidance from a trusted mentor. You don't have to go it alone. With the help of your network, you will find any challenge can be met with the right support.

10

THE GIFT OF WORK

W hen my mother was a little girl, she saw three choices for her future: she could be a teacher, a nurse, or a secretary. She chose secretary because she had a vague idea of what the role entailed (mostly from TV) and a subtle intuition that she might have a knack for it.

From as early as I can remember, my parents always told me I could be anything I wanted—and I believed it! But when my mom was a kid, career opportunities weren't quite as plentiful.

She married young, which was not unusual for that time, and had a baby a year later. She had to work to help make ends meet. Luckily, as she suspected, her personality was very well-suited for the secretarial role; she had great attention to detail, remarkable organizational skills, and unflappable poise. But in those early years, her job was little more than a necessary paycheck.

As time went by, things changed for my mom. She got a divorce and became the sole provider for her son (my older brother). Work became more essential. Though it was hard, she managed to support her little family on her own, and still somehow managed to have a life. During this time, she also met my father —or rather, she re-met him at their ten-year high school reunion.

After a brief courtship, they got married. Some more time passed, and my sister and I arrived. My father was in the military then, so mom had her hands full moving us around the country on a fairly frequent basis. We even spent a year in Japan when I was only four years old. That unflappable poise sure came in handy then!

By the time I started elementary school, we were able to settle down in California. At that point, my mom didn't *need* a job— she wanted one. Being a mother and a military wife certainly qualified as work, but she wanted something else too. Something of her own.

So, she went back to the role she knew so well; she became a secretary. This time, she joined the legal field and ended up staying there until her retirement, which is quite a feat when you're working with attorneys! Looking at it now, it's clear she did, indeed, achieve partnership status with the people she supported. In fact, when one of the lawyers decided to leave and start her own firm, she asked my mother to go with her. *That's* the kind of long-term, mutually beneficial partnership so many admins crave.

Of course, I knew none of that at the time. All I knew was that, when I went to school, she went to work. Every day, I watched her get ready—pinning her hair back in a sophisticated French twist, putting on pantyhose and heels. I would go visit her in the office and marvel at the enormous, beautiful desk she sat behind.

In my eyes, she was living the dream. My mother was my first, and most influential, career role model.

By this time, my father had retired from the military and become a commercial airline pilot. I was definitely influenced by him as well: his work ethic, drive, and focus were unparalleled. I like to think I have a bit of that in me too.

Here's my point in all of this: Work is so important for so many reasons, and those reasons may change throughout our lives, just as my mother experienced.

Sometimes, work is just that thing you do to make ends meet. But it can also be about creating an identity of your own, being a role model for your kids, and being a provider.

Personally, I believe work saved my life. I know that sounds dramatic, so let me explain.

When I was sixteen years old, I decided I didn't want to go to school anymore.

Just to be clear: I *do* have a high school diploma, and I also have a bachelor's degree from a state university in California.

But at sixteen, my future, especially as it related to education, was in serious jeopardy.

You see, at the time, I was in the midst of a difficult period. Teen years are never easy, I know, but I had been through a few particularly tough situations and was struggling to cope. As a result, I found myself making a lot of bad decisions, including this whopper: I wanted to quit school.

Thankfully, I was presented with another option: independent study. Through this program, I could attend school for one day a week to meet with my teachers, take tests, and hand in homework assignments. Everything else would happen on my own.

Miraculously, my parents agreed to it under one condition: I had to work. They didn't want me getting into more trouble with all that extra time on my hands.

For the last two years of high school, I attended independent study and held a number of different jobs, sometimes more than one at a time. I worked at a movie theater, a vitamin store, a clothing shop, and (for a brief period), I bussed tables at a restaurant.

I say work saved my life because it's where I found much-needed healing during this time. Holding a job and working real hours taught me responsibility and humility. It gave me a place to channel my energy, instead of turning perpetually inward. I made new friends at work—people I never would have met at school. And oddly, many of us were going through similar struggles.

Work gave me the confidence I needed to finish high school and then go to college 500 miles away from my hometown.

Again, work is so important for so many reasons. Sometimes, it's just a good way to stay out of trouble. But it can also be about social connection and personal discovery.

As an adult, work has always been a big part of my life. Quite honestly, for a while, it was *the biggest* part of my life. I devoted the majority of my time, energy, and attention to my career, and then to my business. I was so passionate (obsessed, really), I didn't recognize how unhealthy my work habits had become.

Today, age and experience have helped me gain a little perspective. I have a family of my own now, and I know they rightly deserve my time, energy, and attention too. I have to balance the work I love to do with the needs of the people I love.

Wow, what a gift to have this kind of struggle in my life!

This is the core message that lies at the center of everything I do: Work is a gift. It's one of many we receive in life.

This is something I've always intuitively known, but my sister is actually the one who helped me articulate it.

She's another one of my personal career role models. She has more of my dad in her—she's tough as nails and not afraid to roll up her sleeves and get messy if that's what the job takes.

Several years ago, my sister joined Arc Thrift Stores; today, she is the Vice President of Marketing there. Arc is a charitable organization which helps fund programs for people with intellectual and developmental disabilities. A primary mission of Arc is to help integrate people with disabilities into the community through employment. In their thrift stores, you will find many people with special needs, all eager to help you find what you need. Arc helps people with disabilities live rich and meaningful lives, part of which involves having a job—a place to go each day where you get to contribute and provide value to others.

Sometimes, work is about so much more than the actual work being done. It's about independence, and purpose, and service.

My sister's passion for this organization is truly contagious. When I first came to understand what they were doing, I was deeply impacted. While I felt inspired, I also felt profoundly guilty.

How often do I take work for granted? How often do I complain that I *have* to go to work, while others would do anything to *get* to? How often do I see work as a burden rather than a privilege?

Those of us lucky enough to have experienced this thing called work for a while can easily lose sight of our good fortune. We spend more time thinking about what we want, rather than appreciating what we already have—and really, we already have so much.

It's not wrong to want more—the better job, the promotion, the raise—and to work hard for it. But, at the same time, we can't forget the importance of gratitude.

I learned long ago that gratitude is not a feeling or a thought; it's an action. Our behaviors demonstrate our gratitude. If you're grateful for your house, are you taking care of it? If you're grateful for your family, is it evident in your actions?

What can we do to demonstrate gratitude for our work? Here are my thoughts: We can show up every day ready to give it our best. We can focus on possibility instead of negativity, and we can try to be the best version of ourselves.

Work is important, but it's not everything. It's an opportunity, every day, to see what we're made of—and to maybe even make ourselves a little better in the process.

I have long felt that my career is a gift I don't deserve. My job now is to appreciate it and use what I have for the good of others, to help them experience this gift as well.

As you go on from here, I hope you will remember that work can, indeed, be a gift in your life too, if you remain open to receiving it. You deserve it, just like I do. We all do.

ABOUT THE AUTHOR

Chrissy Scivicque is a certified Project Management Professional (PMP) and certified Professional Career Manager (PCM). She is an author, in-demand presenter and international speaker known for engaging, entertaining, educating and empowering audiences of all sizes and backgrounds. She is also a very proud former administrative professional and trusted PACE Certification training partner.

Chrissy is also the founder of Eat Your Career, a popular website devoted to "helping you create a *nourishing* professional life." You can learn more about Chrissy and sign up to attend her free monthly training webinars by visiting www. EatYourCareer.com.

AN EXCERPT FROM "THE PROACTIVE PROFESSIONAL"

BY CHRISSY SCIVICQUE, PMP, PCM

As a professional, you've probably experienced any number of "bad days." Maybe they went something like this…

- You sit down for a meeting with colleagues and the conversation is totally over your head. Apparently, everyone else did some pre-meeting research on their own—and some even made notes for discussion! As your colleagues jump right into business, you struggle to get up to speed.

- You're hosting an important training session online but, as you go to log in, you realize your computer system is missing a critical application required to launch the meeting. It takes 25 minutes and a phone call to tech support before you're finally able to get started. By that point, your participants have already given up, and you have to reschedule the training.

- You put off an important project, knowing it shouldn't take long to complete. However, as the deadline approaches, you encounter tons of unexpected setbacks and delays. Before you know it, the deadline has passed and you're left trying to explain what happened.

What do all these situations have in common?

First, they're typical in today's working world, so don't beat yourself up if they hit close to home. Secondly, they're frustrating, stressful, embarrassing, and potentially career damaging. But here's the good news: Situations like these are also completely within your control.

If you've ever experienced something similar to any of the "bad day" scenarios above, you likely also experienced a moment of clarity where you thought to yourself, "I wish I had done something different *before*..." A month ago, a week ago, an hour ago. If only you had prepped for the meeting, tested the technology, started the project sooner...

If only you had spent a little time in the past preparing for the possibilities of the future, your present would be a whole lot better.

With the benefit of hindsight, it's easy to see the problems that arise when you procrastinate and fail to think ahead. These kinds of situations are telltale signs of professionals who are always playing "catch up"—a game that ensures they'll never get ahead and keeps them constantly blindsided by the events and circumstances life throws their way.

The fascinating part is that most of these things are predictable and preventable—or at the very least, made more manageable—with the help of a skillset called "proactivity." Being proactive gives us the power to not only deal more effectively with life, but to actually take an active role in creating it.

Pretty amazing stuff.

The situations described above are relatively insignificant. Most people would find them irritating but would likely recover quickly. I could share many other stories that are far more serious.

Take, for example, my former client Julie who, after 16 years working for the same organization, arrived at work one day to discover her department and her job had been eliminated. Suddenly unemployed at 53 years old, Julie couldn't even find a copy of her old, outdated resume. When she came to me, her skills were nearly obsolete for her field (she hadn't engaged in any professional development in years) and her network had shrunk to include only a handful of former colleagues at the now downsized company. In short, Julie had become complacent and it came back to bite her.

Stories like this sadden me because things didn't have to be so hard for Julie. But I assure you: After this experience and after our work together, Julie will never be "blindsided" again. She will always be well positioned for her future, whatever that may bring. From now on, she will always be the driver of her own destiny.

Obviously, we don't always know what the future holds and we can't always stop bad things from happening. But we can always make smart decisions today to prepare for the possibilities of the future, and we can take an active role in creating the kind of future we want.

When you're trapped in the tyranny of today, focused solely on the here and now, it can be hard to break out of the cycle. Like Julie, you get comfortable in your day-to-day routine. You're so busy staring down at the road immediately in front of you, that you never bother to look around and make sure you're still on the right path. You begin to believe you know exactly what to expect, even though you really have no idea. You fail to adjust for changes ahead and as a result, you're constantly caught off guard by every little bump or curve in the road.

I presume you're reading this book because you don't like that feeling. Perhaps you're also unhappy with the results you're getting. Put another way: the road you're on isn't leading to the right place and the journey itself is pretty tedious.

Learning to be proactive doesn't mean the road will always be smooth. Bumps and curves will still happen, but you'll be more prepared when they do. More importantly, you'll discover that you're actually even in charge of them. **When you're proactive, your choices and actions dictate the path—not the other way around.**

If this sounds a bit abstract, don't worry. All the pieces of the puzzle will fall into place, I assure you. When they do, that feeling of "playing catch-up" will disappear. You'll feel more empowered and more in control. And you'll finally get ahead at work and in life.

～

The Proactive Professional: How to Stop Playing Catch Up and Start Getting Ahead at Work (and in Life!) is available on Amazon.

ALSO BY CHRISSY SCIVICQUE, PMP, PCM

The Proactive Professional

The Invisibility Cure

The Build Your Professional Development Plan Workbook

Available Exclusively on EatYourCareer.com

Personal Branding for Professional Success

Resume & Cover Letter Toolkit

Rock Your Interview

Build Your Professional Portfolio

Networking Naturally

Guide to Goal Setting & Goal Getting

Modern Business Etiquette

The Career Success Library

An affordable, convenient, on-demand learning center for career-minded professionals

www.MyCareerLibrary.com

Made in the USA
Coppell, TX
03 February 2023

12125363R00136